GoodFood
201 Perfect cakes and bakes

GoodFood
201
Perfect cakes and bakes

BOOKS

10 9 8 7 6 5 4 3 2 1

Published in 2011 by BBC Books, an imprint of Ebury Publishing.
A Random House Group Company
This edition published in 2012 for Index Books Ltd
Photographs © BBC Magazines 2011
Recipes © BBC Magazines 2011
Book design © Woodlands Books Ltd 2011

The Random House Group Limited Reg. No. 954009

Addresses for companies within the Random House Group
can be found at www.randomhouse.co.uk

A CIP catalogue record for this book is available from the
British Library.

The Random House Group Limited supports The Forest
Stewardship Council®(FSC®), the leading international forest
certification organisation. Our books carrying the FSC
label are printed on FSC® certified paper. FSC is the only forest
certification scheme endorsed by the leading environmental
organisations,including Greenpeace. Our paper procurement
Policy can be found at www.randomhouse.co.uk/environment

Project editor: Laura Higginson
Designer: Kathryn Gammon

Colour origination by Dot Gradations Ltd, UK
Printed and bound in China by C&C Offset Printing Co., Ltd

To buy books by your favourite authors and register for offers,
visit www.rbooks.co.uk

Contents

Introduction

In recent years, homebaking has enjoyed a surge in popularity, and it's not hard to see why. When you make your own cake or bake you know exactly what's in it, the basic ingredients are not expensive and baking is highly satisfying and creative, too. Whether you want a cake recipe for the family to enjoy at the weekend or a special-occasion recipe for a birthday (try our *Chocolate birthday cake* on page 68), we hope there is something to suit everyone in this book.

We've collected some of our most popular baking recipes here, such as *Mango, banana and coconut cake* (page 18) and *Seriously rich chocolate cake* (page 40). We have also included a range of ideas from impressive cakes or themed ideas for celebrations, to classic teatime cakes and pastries.

There are also tarts and bakes that double as desserts, and family staples such as traybakes, biscuits and bars. Try *Almond and chocolate torte with apricot cream* (page 36), as a dinner-party dessert that requires little fuss, or *Granola bars* (page 154) for an after-school treat packed with nourishing seeds and nuts. Our *Spider web chocolate fudge muffins* (page 108) are always a popular Halloween choice – and not just with children! Or if you want something more grown-up try *Raspberry coffee time muffins* (page 90) or *Pistachio, orange and oat crumbles* (page 122).

If you're new to baking, don't be put off by the equipment required. You don't need much to get you started. Pick a simple recipe such as *Banana nut brownies* (page 56) or *Devonshire honey cake* (page 30). You will need a large mixing bowl, a wooden spoon and a reliable set of scales. An electric whisk isn't required for either of these recipes but an inexpensive, handheld whisk is useful to make a light cake mix quickly and easily. You do need the right-size cake tin, otherwise your cake mix may rise over the sides of the tin or may come out too flat. The key to foolproof baking is to always weigh ingredients, don't guess quantities, and follow the method and temperature instructions. Happy baking!

Notes and conversion tables

NOTES ON THE RECIPES
• Eggs are large in the UK and Australia and extra large in America unless stated otherwise.
• Wash fresh produce before preparation.
• Recipes contain nutritional analyses for 'sugar', which means the total sugar content including all natural sugars in the ingredients, unless otherwise stated.

OVEN TEMPERATURES

Gas	°C	°C Fan	°F	Oven temp.
¼	110	90	225	Very cool
½	120	100	250	Very cool
1	140	120	275	Cool or slow
2	150	130	300	Cool or slow
3	160	140	325	Warm
4	180	160	350	Moderate
5	190	170	375	Moderately hot
6	200	180	400	Fairly hot
7	220	200	425	Hot
8	230	210	450	Very hot
9	240	220	475	Very hot

APPROXIMATE LIQUID CONVERSIONS

metric	imperial	AUS	US
50ml	2fl oz	¼ cup	¼ cup
125ml	4fl oz	½ cup	½ cup
175ml	6fl oz	¾ cup	¾ cup
225ml	8fl oz	1 cup	1 cup
300ml	10fl oz/½ pint	½ pint	1¼ cups
450ml	16fl oz	2 cups	2 cups/1 pint
600ml	20fl oz/1 pint	1 pint	2½ cups
1 litre	35fl oz/1¾ pints	1¾ pints	1 quart

APPROXIMATE WEIGHT CONVERSIONS
• All the recipes in this book list both imperial and metric measurements. Conversions are approximate and have been rounded up or down. Follow one set of measurements only; do not mix the two.
• Cup measurements, which are used by cooks in Australia and America, have not been listed here as they vary from ingredient to ingredient. Kitchen scales should be used to measure dry/solid ingredients.

Good Food are concerned about sustainable sourcing and animal welfare so where possible we use organic ingredients, humanely reared meats, sustainably caught fish, free-range chickens and eggs and unrefined sugar.

SPOON MEASURES
Spoon measurements are level unless otherwise specified.
• 1 teaspoon (tsp) = 5ml
• 1 tablespoon (tbsp) = 15ml
• 1 Australian tablespoon = 20ml (cooks in Australia should measure 3 teaspoons where 1 tablespoon is specified in a recipe)

Whole orange cake, page 17

Large cakes

Blueberry cheesecake gateau

This tall cake is spectacular, easy to make and keeps for up to one day in the fridge.

TAKES 1¼ HOURS, PLUS 30 MINUTES DECORATING • SERVES 12

225g/8oz self-raising flour
1 tsp baking powder
200g/7oz caster sugar
200g/7oz butter, softened
4 large eggs
2 tsp vanilla extract
1 tbsp milk
FOR THE ICING AND DECORATION
400g/14oz medium-fat soft cheese
grated zest 2 limes and juice 1 lime
100g/3½oz icing sugar
200g/7oz blueberries

1 Heat the oven to 180C/160C fan/gas 4. Butter and line the base of a deep 18cm/7in round cake tin.
2 Put the flour, baking powder, sugar, butter, eggs and vanilla into a large bowl and beat with an electric mixer on low speed until everything is mixed together. Increase the speed and whisk for 2 minutes. Stir in the milk.
3 Spoon the mixture into the tin and level the top. Bake the cake for about 50–60 minutes, until the cake springs back when lightly pressed, cool, then split into three layers.
4 Beat the cheese until soft, then beat in the lime zest and juice and the icing sugar. Sandwich the cake back together with two thirds of the cheese mixture, and spread the rest on the top. Arrange the blueberries in tight circles around the top of the cake.

PER SERVING 380 kcals, protein 8g, carbs 43g, fat 21g, sat fat 9g, fibre 1g, added sugar 27g, salt 0.69g

Fresh cherry and almond cake

This crumbly cake is a terrific way to enjoy fresh cherries.

TAKES 1½ HOURS • SERVES 8

140g/5oz whole blanched almonds
250g/9oz self-raising flour
140g/5oz butter, cut into small pieces and softened
140g/5oz caster sugar
2 eggs, beaten
125ml/4fl oz milk
300g/10oz fresh cherries, stoned and patted dry
25g/1oz flaked almonds

1 Heat the oven to 180C/160C fan/gas 4. Butter and line the base of a 20cm/8in round, deep cake tin. Put the blanched almonds in a small pan and heat gently, shaking occasionally, until golden brown (about 10 minutes). Cool, then whizz in a food processor until finely ground.
2 Tip the flour into a bowl and stir in the ground almonds. Rub in the butter until the mixture is crumbly. Stir in the sugar, then add the eggs, milk and cherries; mix until combined, but don't overmix.
3 Spoon into the prepared tin and smooth the top, then sprinkle the flaked almonds on top. Bake for 1 hour 10 minutes until the cake is golden on top and firm to the touch. Cool in the tin for 10 minutes, then turn out on to a wire rack to cool. Eat within 3 days.

PER SERVING 474 kcals, protein 10g, carbs 48g, fat 28g, sat fat 11g, fibre 2.8g, added sugar 18g, salt 0.69g

Fresh cherry and almond cake

Blueberry cheesecake gateau

Raspberry and blueberry lime drizzle cake

Wonderfully moist and fruity, this cake is a teatime favourite.

TAKES 1 HOUR AND 25 MINUTES • SERVES 12

225g/8oz butter, softened
225g/8oz golden caster sugar
4 eggs
250g/9oz self-raising flour, sifted with a pinch of salt
grated zest and juice 2 limes
25g/1oz ground almonds
100g/3½oz each blueberries and raspberries
FOR THE SYRUP
8 tbsp lime juice (about 4 limes)
grated zest 1 lime
140g/5oz golden caster sugar

1 Heat the oven to 180C/160C fan/gas 4. Line the base and sides of a 20cm/8in square cake tin and butter the paper.
2 Cream the butter and sugar together until light. Gradually beat in the eggs, adding a little of the flour towards the end to prevent curdling. Beat in the lime zest, then fold in the rest of the flour and almonds. Fold in about 3 tablespoons of lime juice, giving a good dropping consistency. Fold in three quarters of the blueberries and raspberries, and turn into the prepared tin. Smooth, then scatter the remaining fruit on top. Bake for about 1 hour or until firm.
3 Gently heat the lime juice, zest and sugar in a saucepan, without allowing to bubble. While the cake is still hot, prick it all over with a skewer then spoon the syrup over it.

PER SERVING 370 kcals, protein 5g, carbs 49g, fat 19g, sat fat 10g, fibre 1g, added sugar 32g, salt 0.61g

St Lucia banana cake

This cake conjures up the taste of the Caribbean.

TAKES 1 HOUR 5 MINUTES • SERVES 12

350g/12oz self-raising flour
1 tsp bicarbonate of soda
2 tsp ground mixed spice
175g/6oz light muscovado sugar
4 eggs
200ml/7fl oz sunflower oil
2 bananas, mashed
100g/3½oz pineapple, very finely chopped
finely grated rind and juice 1 orange
100g pack walnuts, roughly chopped
FOR THE FROSTING
2 x 200g tubs medium-fat soft cheese, at room temperature
200g/7oz icing sugar
50g/2oz honey-coated banana chips

1 Heat the oven to 180C/160C fan/gas 4. Butter and line two 20cm/8in sandwich tins. Sift the flour into a large bowl with the soda, mixed spice and sugar.
2 Whisk the eggs and the oil until smooth. Stir the egg mixture into the flour with the bananas, pineapple, orange rind and juice and walnuts; stir well. Divide between the prepared tins. Bake for 45 minutes until risen and firm. Cool for 10 minutes, then remove from the tins, peel off the paper and leave to cool completely.
3 Beat the soft cheese until smooth. Gradually add the icing sugar to give a smooth frosting. Spread half the frosting over one cake. Put the other cake on top. Spread over the remaining icing, swirling it with a palette knife. Sprinkle over the banana chips.

PER SERVING 545 kcals, protein 10g, carbs 64g, fat 30g, sat fat 3g, fibre 2g, added sugar 32g, salt 0.66g

Raspberry and blueberry lime drizzle cake

St Lucia banana cake

Lemon polenta cake with rosemary syrup

A bold, unusual dessert that marries fruit and herbs.

TAKES 1 HOUR 5 MINUTES • SERVES 8–10

175g/6oz polenta
50g/2oz plain flour
1½ tsp baking powder
¼ tsp salt
5 tbsp natural yogurt
5 tbsp groundnut oil, plus extra for greasing
grated rind 2 lemons, plus 2 tbsp fresh
    lemon juice
2 eggs, plus 2 egg whites
400g/14oz caster sugar
2 sprigs fresh rosemary, plus extra sprigs
    to decorate
fresh raspberries and Greek yogurt, to serve

1 Heat the oven to 180C/160C fan/gas 4. Sift the polenta, flour, baking powder and salt into a bowl. Tip the yogurt, oil, lemon rind and juice into a jug; stir to combine.
2 Beat the eggs and egg whites with half the sugar until creamy. Beat in the yogurt mixture until smooth, then fold in the dry ingredients. Pour the batter into a 1.2 litre/2 pint lightly oiled, lined loaf tin. Bake for 40–45 minutes or until a skewer inserted into the centre comes out clean.
3 Put the remaining sugar in a pan with 200ml/7fl oz water and the rosemary sprigs. Bring to the boil, then simmer for 10 minutes. Cool completely, then strain.
4 Cool the cake on a wire rack for 15 minutes. Prick the top and drizzle over half the rosemary syrup. Serve decorated with the rosemary sprigs, and the raspberries, yogurt and extra syrup.

PER SERVING (for eight) 390 kcals, protein 6g, carbs 74g, fat 10g, sat fat 2g, fibre 1g, added sugar 53g, salt 0.43g

Rhubarb and orange cake

This is good warm, as a pudding with whipped cream, or cold, as a moist, fruity cake.

TAKES 1 HOUR 25 MINUTES, PLUS 1 HOUR STANDING • SERVES 6–8

350g/12oz prepared rhubarb, cut into
    4cm/1½in lengths
200g/7oz golden caster sugar
finely grated zest and juice ½ small orange
140g/5oz butter, softened
2 eggs, beaten
½ tsp baking powder
85g/3oz self-raising flour
100g/3½oz ground almonds
FOR THE TOPPING
25g/1oz butter, melted
25g/1oz light muscovado sugar
finely grated zest ½ small orange
50g/2oz slivered almonds
icing sugar, for dusting

1 Mix the rhubarb with 50g/2oz of the caster sugar and the orange zest. Set aside for 1 hour, stirring once or twice.
2 Heat the oven to 190C/170C fan/gas 5. Butter and line the base of a deep 23cm/9in round cake tin. Cream the butter and remaining caster sugar. Add the eggs, baking powder, flour and ground almonds. Beat gently, but do not overmix. Stir in the orange juice, spoon into the tin, and level. Drain the rhubarb and spoon over the mixture. Bake for 25 minutes. Meanwhile, combine the butter, sugar, zest and almonds.
3 Reduce the oven to 180C/160C fan/gas 4. Sprinkle the topping over the cake and return to the oven for 15–20 minutes or until firm. Cool in the tin, then transfer to a wire rack. Dust with icing sugar.

PER SERVING (for six) 548 kcals, protein 9g, carbs 44g, fat 39g, sat fat 16g, fibre 3g, added sugar 41g, salt 0.74g

Lemon polenta cake with rosemary syrup

Rhubarb and orange cake

Fresh cherry cake with a hint of cinnamon

Make this cake the day before a picnic – it's sturdy and travels well.

TAKES 1 HOUR 5 MINUTES • SERVES 8

140g/5oz self-raising flour
½ tsp ground cinnamon
50g/2oz golden caster sugar
1 egg
4 tbsp milk
85g/3oz butter, melted
350g/12oz juicy, ripe cherries, stalks and
    stones removed
icing sugar, for dusting
FOR THE TOPPING
25g/1oz plain flour
¼ tsp ground cinnamon
25g/1oz golden caster sugar
25g/1oz butter, diced and softened

1 Heat the oven to 180C/160C fan/gas 4. Butter and line the base of a 20cm/8in round cake tin. Sift the flour, cinnamon and sugar into a bowl. Make a well and add the egg, milk and melted butter. Combine and beat to make a thick, smooth mixture. Spoon into the tin and smooth. Scatter the cherries over the mixture and gently press them in.
2 Tip all the topping ingredients into a bowl. Rub in the butter to make a crumb-like mixture, then work until it comes together in pea-size pieces. Scatter this over the cherries.
3 Bake for 30–35 minutes until a skewer pushed into the centre comes out clean. Leave in the tin until cool enough to handle, then tip on to a wire rack until completely cold.

PER SERVING 247 kcals, protein 3g, carbs 32g, fat 12g, sat fat 7g, fibre 1g, added sugar 12g, salt 0.46g

Apple and cinnamon cake

Serve this warm from the oven as a tasty dessert, or cold for a picnic or lunchbox treat.

TAKES 1 HOUR • SERVES 8–10

250g/9oz self-raising flour
1 tsp ground cinnamon
1 tsp baking powder
100g/3½oz light muscovado sugar
175g/6oz sultanas or raisins
125ml/4fl oz sunflower oil
2 eggs, beaten
125ml/4fl oz apple juice
2 dessert apples (not peeled), grated
25g/1oz slivered or flaked almonds
icing sugar, for dusting

1 Heat the oven to 180C/160C fan/gas 4. Line a 23cm/9in round deep cake tin with baking paper. Sift the flour into a bowl with the cinnamon and baking powder, then stir in the sugar and sultanas or raisins. Make a well in the centre and stir in the oil, eggs, apple juice and grated apple until well mixed.
2 Pour the mixture into the tin, scatter with almonds, then bake for 40–45 minutes until firm in the centre or a skewer inserted into the middle comes out clean. Leave to cool in the tin for about 5 minutes, then turn out and cool on a wire rack. Dust with icing sugar.

PER SERVING (for ten) 342 kcals, protein 6g, carbs 46g, fat 16g, sat fat 2g, fibre 2g, added sugar 10g, salt 0.46g

Raspberry and almond madeira cake

This tasty cake can be made in advance, but is best eaten within 2–3 days.

TAKES 1½ HOURS • SERVES 8

175g/6oz butter, softened
175g/6oz caster sugar
1 tsp vanilla extract
3 eggs, lightly beaten
50g/2oz flaked almonds
grated zest 1 orange
100g/3½oz plain flour, sifted
100g/3½oz self-raising flour, sifted
2 tbsp milk
200g/7oz raspberries, fresh or frozen
icing sugar, for dusting

1 Heat the oven to 160C/140C fan/gas 3. Line a deep 20cm/8in cake tin. Cream the butter and sugar. Beat in the vanilla, then gradually beat in the eggs.

2 Set aside a few almonds. Crumble the rest and stir them and the zest into the batter. Fold in the sifted flours and milk, then fold in all but eight of the raspberries.

3 Put the mixture in the tin and level, then arrange the remaining raspberries on top. Sprinkle the remaining almonds over the top, and bake for 1¼ hours. Cool in the tin for 10 minutes, then cool on a rack. Dust with icing sugar.

PER SERVING 410 kcals, protein 7g, carbs 45g, fat 24g, sat fat 12g, fibre 2g, added sugar 24g, salt 0.61g

Whole orange cake

The juicy flavour of a whole orange goes into this cake.

TAKES 1 HOUR 45 MINUTES • SERVES 8–10

1 small orange
140g/5oz caster sugar
3 eggs
85g/3oz self-raising flour
100g/3½oz ground almonds
50g/2oz butter, melted
FOR THE ICING
85g/3oz icing sugar
juice 1 small sweet orange (or enough to make a smooth pouring icing)
crème fraîche, to serve (optional)

1 Put the orange in a pan and cover with cold water. Bring to the boil, cover and simmer for 1 hour. Remove the orange and cool.

2 Heat the oven to 180C/160C fan/gas 4. Butter and line the base of a 20cm/8in round, deep cake tin. Roughly chop the cooked orange, discarding the pips. Whizz in a food processor until smooth. Whisk the sugar and eggs until light and fluffy.

3 Sift the flour and ground almonds on to the egg mixture. Using a large metal spoon, fold gently, then add the orange purée and melted butter. Fold in gently until just mixed. Pour the cake mixture into the prepared tin. Bake for 40–45 minutes until the cake is brown and springs back when lightly pressed. Cool in the tin for 5 minutes. Mix the icing sugar and juice together, drizzle, and serve with crème fraîche.

PER SERVING (for eight) 307 kcals, protein 6g, carbs 41g, fat 14g, sat fat 4g, fibre 2g, added sugar 30g, salt 0.29g

Lemon flower cake

A perfect cake for Easter from Orlando Murrin, editor of Good Food *Magazine.*

TAKES 50 MINUTES, PLUS 2 HOURS DRYING TIME • SERVES 8–10

FOR THE SUGAR-FROSTED FLOWERS
selection of pansies, calendulas and other seasonal edible flowers
1 egg white, very lightly beaten
caster sugar, for coating the flowers

FOR THE CAKE
175g/6oz butter, softened
175g/6oz caster sugar
3 eggs
175g/6oz self-raising flour
1½ tsp baking powder
finely grated zest 1 lemon

FOR THE TOPPING AND FILLING
85g/3oz caster sugar, plus extra for sprinkling
juice 1½ lemons
250g tub mascarpone

1 Brush the flower petals with the egg white, then sprinkle with the caster sugar. Shake off any excess. Leave for 2 hours to dry.

2 Heat the oven to 190C/170C fan/gas 5. Lightly butter and line two 18cm/7in round sandwich tins. Put all the cake ingredients in a large mixing bowl, add a tablespoon of warm water and beat until smooth. Divide the mixture between the tins, smooth, then bake for 25–30 minutes until the cakes spring back when pressed.

3 Mix the topping sugar with the juice of one lemon. Prick the cakes and spoon the topping mixture over. Cool, then transfer to a wire rack. Add the remaining lemon juice to the mascarpone and use this mixture to layer the cakes. Sprinkle caster sugar lightly over the top, then decorate with the flowers.

PER SERVING (for eight) 538 kcals, protein 6g, carbs 54g, fat 35g, sat fat 21g, fibre 1g, added sugar 35g, salt 1.12g

Mango, banana and coconut cake

Buy your mangoes a couple of days ahead to ensure they are fully ripe.

TAKES 55 MINUTES • SERVES 10

1 medium, ripe mango
2 ripe bananas
1 tsp vanilla extract
225g/8oz butter, softened
140g/5oz light muscovado sugar
2 eggs, beaten
50g/2oz desiccated coconut
225g/8oz self-raising flour
½ tsp bicarbonate of soda
1 tsp ground mixed spice

FOR THE FILLING
200g packet full-fat soft cheese
2 tsp lemon juice
25g/1oz icing sugar, plus extra for dusting

1 Heat the oven 160C/140C fan/gas 3. Butter and line the bases of two round 20cm/8in sandwich tins. Peel, stone and chop the mango, then purée the flesh. Mash the bananas, then mix in half the mango purée and the vanilla.

2 Beat together the butter and sugar until light and fluffy. Beat in the eggs, a little at a time, then stir in the banana mixture, and the coconut. Sift in the flour, bicarbonate of soda and spice, then fold in lightly. Divide the mixture between the tins and smooth. Bake for 30–35 minutes. Cool in the tins for 5 minutes, then turn out on to a wire rack.

3 Beat together the filling ingredients, then stir in the reserved mango. Spread one cake with the filling. Put the other cake on top and dust lightly with icing sugar.

PER SERVING 468 kcals, protein 5g, carbs 42g, fat 32g, sat fat 21g, fibre 2g, added sugar 17g, salt 0.83g

Mango, banana and coconut cake

Lemon flower cake

Almond cake with clementines

This cake is very light, and the apricots add a juicy note – a brilliant special-occasion dessert.

TAKES 1 HOUR 50 MINUTES • SERVES 8

100g/3½oz ready-to-eat dried apricots
175ml/6fl oz clementine juice (about 6–8 clementines)
100g/3½oz butter, softened
100g/3½oz golden caster sugar
2 eggs
50g/2oz self-raising flour
175g/6oz ground almonds
½ tsp vanilla extract
2 tbsp slivered almonds
icing sugar, for dusting
8 clementines in syrup (from a jar) and thick cream or Greek yogurt, to serve

1 Heat the oven to 180C/160C fan/gas 4. Butter and line the base of a 20cm/8in round cake tin. Finely chop the apricots and put in a pan with the clementine juice. Bring to the boil, then gently simmer for 5 minutes. Leave to cool.
2 Beat the butter, sugar, eggs and flour in a bowl for 2 minutes until light and fluffy, then fold in the ground almonds, vanilla and apricots along with their juices.
3 Turn the mixture into the prepared tin and smooth. Scatter the slivered almonds on top. Bake for 40–50 minutes until firm. Cool in the tin for 5 minutes, then turn out and cool on a wire rack. Dust the cake with icing sugar. Slice, and put a wedge on each plate with a clementine. Spoon the syrup over the cake and fruit. Serve with the cream or yogurt.

PER SERVING 291 kcals, protein 6g, carbs 27g, fat 19g, sat fat 8g, fibre 2g, added sugar 15g, salt 0.36g

Citrus poppy seed cake

This treat can be stored in the fridge for up to 3 days.

TAKES 1 HOUR 5 MINUTES • SERVES 10

175g/6oz butter, softened
175g/6oz caster sugar
3 eggs, beaten
250g/9oz self-raising flour
50g/2oz poppy seeds
grated rind 2 oranges
grated rind 2 lemons
4 rounded tbsp natural yogurt
FOR THE TOPPING
250g tub mascarpone
grated rind and juice 1 small orange
3 tbsp orange or lemon curd
grated rind 1 lemon

1 Heat the oven to 150C/130C fan/gas 2. Butter and line the base of a deep 20cm/8in round cake tin. Using a wooden spoon, beat together the butter, sugar, eggs, flour, poppy seeds, citrus rinds and yogurt until smooth.
2 Spread the mixture in the tin and bake for 45–50 minutes until just firm. Cool in the tin for 10 minutes, then turn out and cool on a wire rack. Peel off the paper.
3 Meanwhile, mix the mascarpone with enough orange juice to make a spreadable icing. Lightly swirl in the curd to give a marbled effect. Roughly spread over the top and sides of the cake, and scatter the grated citrus rind over the top to decorate.

PER SERVING 483 kcals, protein 7g, carbs 48g, fat 31g, sat fat 11g, fibre 2g, added sugar 18g, salt 0.74g

Almond cake with clementines

Citrus poppy seed cake

Strawberry and cinnamon torte

The perfect crumbly dessert for a summer Sunday lunch or dinner.

TAKES 1¼ HOURS • SERVES 6–8

175g/6oz ground almonds
175g/6oz butter, softened
175g/6oz golden caster sugar
175g/6oz self-raising flour
1 tsp ground cinnamon
1 egg, plus 1 egg yolk
450g/1lb strawberries, hulled and sliced
icing sugar, for dusting
whipped double cream mixed with Greek
    yogurt, to serve

1 Heat the oven to 180C/160C fan/gas 4. Butter and line the base of a loose-bottomed 23cm/9in cake tin. In a food processor, mix the ground almonds, butter, sugar, flour, cinnamon, egg and egg yolk until evenly mixed.
2 Tip half the mixture in the tin, and smooth. Spread the strawberries on top. Top with the remaining cake mixture; spread smooth.
3 Bake for 1 hour–1 hour 5 minutes. Check after 40 minutes – if the torte is getting too brown, cover loosely with foil. When cooked, the torte should be slightly risen and dark golden brown.
4 Cool slightly, then remove from the tin. Slide on to a plate and dust with icing sugar. Serve warm, in wedges, with spoonfuls of cream and Greek yogurt.

PER SERVING (for eight) 491 kcals, protein 9g, carbs 45g, fat 32g, sat fat 13g, fibre 3g, added sugar 23g, salt 0.68g

Orange and almond cake

This unconventionally made bittersweet cake freezes beautifully.

TAKES 50 MINUTES • SERVES 12

1 medium orange
175g/6oz butter, softened
175g/6oz light muscovado sugar
3 eggs
175g/6oz self-raising flour
½ tsp bicarbonate of soda
50g/2oz ground almonds
icing sugar, for dredging

1 Heat the oven to 190C/170C fan/gas 5. Butter and line the base of a 23cm/9in round deep cake tin. Cut the whole orange – skin, pith, flesh, the lot – into pieces. Remove any pips, then whizz the orange pieces in a food processor to a finely chopped purée.
2 Tip the butter, sugar, eggs, flour, bicarbonate of soda and almonds into the processor and whizz for 10 seconds, until smooth. Pour into the prepared tin and smooth the top.
3 Bake for 25–30 minutes, until the cake is risen and brown. Allow to cool in the tin for 5 minutes before turning out on to a wire rack. Dredge thickly with icing sugar before serving.

PER SERVING 266 kcals, protein 4g, carbs 29g, fat 16g, sat fat 8g, fibre 1g, added sugar 16g, salt 0.61g

Strawberry and cinnamon torte

Orange and almond cake

Cinnamon nutella cake

Chuck the lot into a bowl, give it a quick beat and it's ready to bake.

TAKES 1½ HOURS • SERVES 12

175g/6oz butter, softened
175g/6oz golden caster sugar
3 eggs
200g/7oz self-raising flour
1 tsp baking powder
2 tsp ground cinnamon
4 tbsp milk
4 rounded tbsp chocolate hazelnut spread
50g/2oz hazelnuts, roughly chopped

1 Heat the oven to 180C/160C fan/gas 4. Butter and line the base of a 20cm/8in round cake tin.
2 Put the butter, sugar, eggs, flour, baking powder, cinnamon and milk into a bowl. Beat until light and fluffy.
3 Tip three quarters of the mixture into the tin, spread it level, then spoon the hazelnut spread on in four blobs. Top with the remaining mixture, swirl a few times with a skewer, then smooth.
4 Sprinkle with the nuts. Bake for 1 hour–1 hour 10 minutes, until risen, nicely browned, feels firm to the touch and springs back when lightly pressed (cover with foil if it starts to brown too quickly). Cool in the tin for 10 minutes, then turn out, peel off the paper and cool on a wire rack.

PER SERVING 320 kcals, protein 5g, carbs 34g, fat 19g, sat fat 8g, fibre 1g, added sugar 20g, salt 0.63g

Carrot, apple and raisin cake

This egg-free cake is a real teatime treat – it's packed with fruit and cinnamon.

TAKES 1 HOUR 40 MINUTES • SERVES 12

225g/8oz self-raising flour
½ tsp baking powder
½ tsp salt
1 tsp ground cinnamon
5 tbsp vegetable oil
grated zest 1 orange plus 4 tbsp juice
140g/5oz light muscovado sugar
140g/5oz finely grated carrot
1 medium eating apple, peeled, cored and grated
85g/3oz raisins
50g/2oz pumpkin seeds
icing sugar, for dusting

1 Heat the oven to 180C/160C fan/gas 4. Butter a 20cm/8in round cake tin. Mix the flour, baking powder, salt and cinnamon together in a large bowl. In a separate bowl mix together the oil, orange juice and sugar.
2 Add the orange mixture to the flour along with the grated carrot and apple, orange zest, raisins and pumpkin seeds, and stir until really well mixed. Spoon into the prepared tin.
3 Bake for 50 minutes–1 hour, until the cake pulls from the side of the tin. Cool on a wire rack before removing from tin. Dust with icing sugar and serve.

PER SERVING 207 kcals, protein 3g, carbs 36g, fat 7g, sat fat 1g, fibre 1g, added sugar 13g, salt 0.47g

Porter cake

A lovely, moist cake that gets even better if left undisturbed in the cake tin for a couple of days.

TAKES 2 HOURS 25 MINUTES • SERVES 12

175g/6oz butter
450g/1lb mixed dried fruit
grated zest and juice 1 orange
175g/6oz light muscovado sugar
200ml/7fl oz porter
1 tsp bicarbonate of soda
3 eggs, beaten
300g/10oz plain flour
2 tsp ground mixed spice
FOR THE TOPPING
2 tbsp flaked almonds
2 tbsp demerara sugar

1 Heat the oven to 150C/130C fan/gas 2. Butter and line the base of a deep 20cm/8in round cake tin. Put the butter, dried fruit, orange zest and juice, sugar and porter in a large pan. Bring slowly to the boil, stirring until the butter has dissolved, then simmer for 15 minutes.
2 Cool for 10 minutes, then stir in the bicarbonate of soda. The mixture will foam up, but don't worry, this is normal.
3 Stir the eggs into the pan, then sift in the flour and spice, and mix well. Pour into the prepared tin, smooth the top with the back of a spoon and sprinkle with the flaked almonds and demerara sugar. Bake for 1¼–1½ hours. Cool in the tin for 15 minutes, then turn out and cool on a wire rack.

PER SERVING 400 kcals, protein 6g, carbs 63g, fat 15g, sat fat 8g, fibre 2g, added sugar 17g, salt 0.69g

Yummy scrummy carrot cake

Light and enticingly moist, this cake keeps for up to a week in a tin.

TAKES 1¼ HOURS • SERVES 15

175g/6oz light muscovado sugar
175ml/6fl oz sunflower oil
3 large eggs, lightly beaten
140g/5oz grated carrot (about 3 medium carrots)
100g/3½oz raisins
grated zest 1 large orange
175g/6oz self-raising flour
1 tsp bicarbonate of soda
1 tsp ground cinnamon
½ tsp grated nutmeg (freshly grated will give you the best flavour)
FOR THE FROSTING
175g/6oz icing sugar
1½–2 tbsp orange juice

1 Heat the oven to 180C/160C fan/gas 4. Oil and line the base and sides of an 18cm/7in square cake tin. Tip the sugar into a large mixing bowl, pour in the oil and add the eggs. Lightly mix, then stir in the grated carrots, raisins and orange zest.
2 Mix the flour, soda and spices, then sift into the bowl. Lightly mix all the ingredients.
3 Pour the mixture into the prepared tin and bake for 40–45 minutes, until it feels firm and springy when you press it in the centre. Cool in the tin for 5 minutes, then turn it out, peel off the paper and cool on a wire rack.
4 Beat together the frosting ingredients in a small bowl until smooth. Set the cake on a serving plate and drizzle the icing over the top. Leave to set, then cut into slices.

PER SERVING 265 kcals, protein 3g, carbs 39g, fat 12g, sat fat 2g, fibre 1g, added sugar 24g, salt 0.41g

Apple cake in a nutshell

An all-in-one cake, topped with fresh apples, then glazed for a beautiful finish.

TAKES 1¼ HOURS • SERVES 12

3 eggs
175g/6oz butter, melted
350g/12oz self-raising flour
2 tsp ground cinnamon
175g/6oz light muscovado sugar
3 medium eating apples, such as Cox's,
    unpeeled and cored
100g/3½oz dates, stoned and cut into pieces
100g/3½oz blanched hazelnuts, roughly
    chopped
3 tbsp apricot compote

1 Heat the oven to 180C/160C fan/gas 4. Butter and line the base of a 20cm/8in cake tin. Beat the eggs into the cooled butter. Put the flour, cinnamon and sugar into a separate bowl, and mix well.

2 Cut two of the apples into chunks. Stir the chunks into the flour with the dates and half of the hazelnuts. Mix well. Pour the egg and butter mixture into the flour mixture and stir gently. Spoon into the tin, and smooth.

3 Cut the remaining apple into thin slices and arrange over the cake. Sprinkle the remaining hazelnuts over the apple slices. Bake for 50 minutes–1 hour, or until a skewer inserted into the centre comes out clean. Cool in the tin for 5 minutes, then turn out on to a wire rack. While the cake is still warm, heat the apricot compote. Brush over the cake, then cool completely.

PER SERVING 377 kcals, protein 6g, carbs 49g, fat 19g, sat fat 8g, fibre 3g, added sugar 15g, salt 0.61g

Soured cream rhubarb squares

These squares are really light, and delicious hot or cold.

TAKES 1 HOUR 20 MINUTES • SERVES 15

100g/3½oz butter, softened
100g/3½oz golden caster sugar
100g/3½oz mixed nuts, roughly chopped
1 tsp ground cinnamon
250g/9oz dark muscovado sugar
1 large egg
225g/8oz plain flour
1 tsp bicarbonate of soda
½ tsp salt
2 x 142ml pots soured cream
300g/10oz rhubarb, cut into 1cm pieces

1 Heat the oven to 180C/160C fan/gas 4. Line a 33 x 23cm/13 x 9in deep baking tin with baking paper. Melt about 15g/½oz of the butter and stir into the caster sugar, nuts and cinnamon in a bowl. Set aside.

2 Beat together the rest of the butter with the muscovado sugar and egg. When smooth and creamy, stir in the flour, bicarbonate of soda, salt and the soured cream. Lastly, stir in the rhubarb.

3 Pour the rhubarb mixture into the prepared tin and sprinkle with the sugar and nut topping. Bake for 30–35 minutes or until a skewer inserted in the centre comes out clean. Serve immediately as a pudding, or leave to cool and cut into squares. Keeps for 4–5 days in an airtight tin.

PER SERVING 277 kcals, protein 4g, carbs 37g, fat 13g, sat fat 7g, fibre 1g, added sugar 24g, salt 0.63g

Soured cream rhubarb squares

Apple cake in a nutshell

Blueberry soured cream cake

Blueberries bake really well in cakes, as their purple skins keep in their juicy centres.

TAKES 1 HOUR 25 MINUTES • SERVES 10

175g/6oz butter, softened
175g/6oz golden caster sugar
3 large eggs
225g/8oz self-raising flour
1 tsp baking powder
2 tsp vanilla extract
142ml pot soured cream
3 x 125g punnets blueberries
FOR THE FROSTING
200g tub soft cheese
100g/3½oz icing sugar

1 Heat the oven to 180C/160C fan/gas 4. Butter and line the base of a 23cm/9in round cake tin. Put the butter, sugar, eggs, flour, baking powder and vanilla in a bowl. Beat for 2–3 minutes until pale and well mixed. Beat in 4 tablespoons soured cream, then stir in half the blueberries.
2 Tip the mixture into the tin and level. Bake for 50 minutes, or until it feels firm to the touch and springs back when lightly pressed. Cool for 10 minutes, then take out of the tin and peel off the paper. Leave to finish cooling.
3 Beat the soft cheese with the icing sugar and the remaining soured cream until smooth and creamy. Spread over the top of the cooled cake and scatter with the remaining blueberries. The cake will keep in the fridge for a couple of days.

PER SERVING 469 kcals, protein 6g, carbs 50g, fat 29g, sat fat 17g, fibre 1g, added sugar 29g, salt 0.93g

Coconut cake

Remind yourself of the lovely, moist flavour of coconut with this nostalgic bake.

TAKES 45 MINUTES • SERVES 8

175g/6oz butter, softened
175g/6oz golden caster sugar
175g/6oz self-raising flour
1½ tsp baking powder
3 eggs, beaten
50g/2oz desiccated coconut
2 tbsp coconut cream, or single cream
FOR THE BUTTERCREAM FILLING AND TOPPING
300g/10oz icing sugar
100g/3½oz butter, softened
3 tbsp coconut cream, or single cream
5 tbsp raspberry jam

1 Heat the oven to 180C/160C fan/gas 4. Butter two 20cm/8in sandwich tins and line the bases with greaseproof paper. Mix the butter, sugar, flour, baking powder and eggs in a food processor for 2–3 minutes until smooth. Gently stir in the coconut and cream.
2 Divide the mixture between the tins and smooth the tops. Bake for 25 minutes until evenly golden and firm. Loosen the edges and leave in the tins for 5 minutes, then turn out on to a wire rack to cool. Peel off the lining paper.
3 Make the buttercream: beat together the icing sugar, butter and cream until smooth. Spread one sponge with the jam. Top with just under half the buttercream and sandwich with the other sponge. Swirl the remaining buttercream on top of the cake.

PER SERVING 410 kcals, protein 9g, carbs 42g, fat 23g, sat fat 13g, fibre 1g, added sugar 14g, salt 1.22g

Coconut cake

Blueberry soured cream cake

Cherry and marzipan cake

A special-occasion cake from Good Food *reader and baker Carrie Hill.*

TAKES 1 HOUR 55 MINUTES • SERVES 12

200g/7oz butter, softened
200g/7oz caster sugar
4 eggs, beaten
200g/7oz self-raising flour
200g/7oz glacé cherries, chopped
100g/3½oz ground almonds
2–3 drops almond extract
250g/9oz marzipan
50g/2oz blanched almonds, halved lengthways
icing sugar, for dusting

1 Heat the oven to 160C/140C fan/gas 3. Butter and line a deep 20cm/8in round cake tin. Beat the butter and sugar in a bowl until light and creamy. Pour in the eggs a little at a time and beat well after each addition. Mix in the flour one third at a time.

2 Fold in the cherries, ground almonds and almond extract until evenly mixed. Spoon half the mixture into the tin.

3 Roll out the marzipan to a 19cm/7½in circle. Lay this on top of the cake mixture in the tin, then cover with the rest of the mixture. Level and scatter the almonds on top.

4 Bake for 1½ hours, or until a skewer inserted in to the centre comes out clean, covering with foil after 1 hour. Leave to cool in the tin for 20 minutes, then turn out on to a wire rack and cool completely. Dust with icing sugar.

PER SERVING 479 kcals, protein 8g, carbs 57g, fat 26g, sat fat 10g, fibre 2g, added sugar 35g, salt 0.57g

Devonshire honey cake

This cake is based on a recipe by food writer Geraldene Holt, who lived in Devon for many years.

TAKES 1½ HOURS • SERVES 12

225g/8oz unsalted butter
250g/9oz clear honey, plus about 2 tbsp extra
    to glaze
100g/3½oz dark muscovado sugar
3 large eggs, beaten
300g/10oz self-raising flour

1 Heat the oven to 160C/140C fan/ gas 3. Butter and line a 20cm/8in round loose-bottomed cake tin. Cut the butter into pieces and drop into a medium pan with the honey and sugar. Melt slowly over a low heat. When liquid, increase the heat under the pan and boil for about 1 minute. Leave to cool.

2 Beat the eggs into the cooled honey mixture using a wooden spoon. Sift the flour into a large bowl and pour in the egg and honey mixture, beating until you have a smooth batter.

3 Pour the mixture into the tin and bake for 50 minutes–1 hour until the cake is well risen, golden brown and springs back when pressed.

4 Turn the cake out on a wire rack. Warm 2 tablespoons honey in a small pan and brush over the top of the cake to glaze, then leave to cool.

PER SERVING 336 kcals, protein 4g, carbs 43g, fat 17g, sat fat 10g, fibre 1g, added sugar 25g, salt 0.29g

Cherry and marzipan cake

Devonshire honey cake

Authentic Yorkshire parkin

This traditional cake for Guy Fawkes night will keep for up to two weeks.

TAKES 1 HOUR 10 MINUTES • SERVES 16

1 egg
3 tbsp milk
175g/6oz golden syrup
100g/3½oz black treacle
85g/3oz light muscovado sugar
225g/8oz butter
100g/3½oz medium oatmeal
250g/9oz plain flour
2 rounded tsp ground ginger
2 tsp bicarbonate of soda

1 Heat the oven to 160C/140C fan/gas 3. Butter a deep 23cm/9in square cake tin and line. Beat the egg and stir in the milk, then set aside.
2 Put the syrup, treacle, sugar and butter in a large pan and heat gently until the sugar has dissolved and the butter has melted. Remove from the heat. Mix together the oatmeal, flour, ginger and bicarbonate of soda, then stir into the syrup mixture, followed by the egg and milk. Combine well.
3 Pour the mixture into the tin and bake for 50 minutes–1 hour until the cake feels firm and a little crusty on top. Leave to cool in the tin, then turn out and peel off the paper. Wrap the parkin in clean greaseproof paper and foil, and leave it for at least 3 days – this allows it to become much softer and stickier.

PER SERVING 261 kcals, protein 3g, carbs 36g, fat 13g, sat fat 8g, fibre 1g, added sugar 18g, salt 0.38g

Raisin spice cake

You can store this cake for up to a week in a tin.

TAKES 1 HOUR 20 MINUTES • SERVES 10–12

FOR THE TOPPING
25g/1oz butter
25g/1oz demerara sugar
1 tsp ground mixed spice
25g/1oz chopped nuts
FOR THE CAKE
175ml/6fl oz unsweetened orange juice
175g/6oz raisins
175g/6oz butter
175g/6oz light muscovado sugar
250g/9oz self-raising flour
1 tsp ground mixed spice
1 tsp ground cinnamon
1 tsp ground ginger
3 eggs, beaten

1 Heat the oven to 160C/140C fan/gas 3. Butter a 23cm/9in ring tin or 20cm/8in round cake tin. Make the topping: chop the butter into the topping ingredients, then sprinkle in the tin.
2 Pour the juice into a pan, then add the raisins, butter and sugar. Bring to the boil, stirring, then simmer for 5 minutes.
3 Lift off the heat; cool for 10 minutes. Sift the flour, mixed spice, cinnamon and ginger into the pan, then add the eggs and mix. Pour into the tin and smooth the top.
4 Bake for 45 minutes until firm. Cool in the tin for 5 minutes, then transfer to a wire rack to cool completely.

PER SERVING (for ten) 408 kcals, protein 6g, carbs 54g, fat 20g, sat fat 11g, fibre 1g, added sugar 20g, salt 0.75g

Olive oil cake

The flavour of the olive oil comes through along with the citrus fruits and the almonds.

TAKES 1 HOUR 25 MINUTES • SERVES 12

1 orange
1 lemon
4 large eggs
100g/3½oz caster sugar
175g/6oz plain flour
1 tbsp baking powder
225ml/8fl oz extra virgin olive oil
100g/3½oz blanched almonds, toasted and
    finely chopped
icing sugar, for dusting

1 Heat the oven to 180C/160C fan/gas 4. Oil and line the base of a 23cm/9in loose-bottomed or springform round cake tin. Put the orange and lemon in a pan and cover with water. Bring to the boil and leave to simmer for 30 minutes until very soft. Drain and cool. Cut away the skin from the white pith and whizz the skin to a puréed paste in a food processor.
2 In a large bowl, beat the eggs with the sugar for 7–8 minutes. Sift the flour, baking powder and a pinch of salt together, then fold lightly into the egg mixture along with the olive oil. Very gently fold in the almonds and puréed fruit skin, but don't overmix.
3 Pour the batter into the tin and bake for 45 minutes. Cool on a wire rack, then dust with icing sugar.

PER SERVING 333 kcals, protein 6g, carbs 25g, fat 24g, sat fat 3g, fibre 1g, added sugar 11g, salt 0.45g

Prune and chocolate torte

Rich with brandy-steeped prunes, this is a cake for real lovers of chocolate.

TAKES 1 HOUR 5 MINUTES, PLUS 30 MINUTES SOAKING TIME • SERVES 8

250g/9oz no-soak prunes, halved
4 tbsp brandy
25g/1oz cocoa powder
100g/3½oz dark chocolate (at least 70% cocoa
    solids), broken into pieces
50g/2oz butter
175g/6oz golden caster sugar
4 large egg whites
85g/3oz plain flour
1 tsp ground cinnamon
lightly whipped cream, or crème fraîche,
    to serve

1 Soak the prunes in brandy for about 30 minutes. Heat the oven to 190C/170C fan/gas 5. Butter a 23cm/9in loose-bottomed cake tin. Put the cocoa, chocolate, butter and 140g/5oz of the sugar in a pan, add 100ml/3½fl oz hot water and gently heat until smooth. Leave to cool slightly.
2 Whisk the egg whites to soft peaks, then gradually whisk in the remaining sugar. Sift the flour and cinnamon over and gently fold in with a metal spoon, until almost combined. Add the chocolate mixture and fold in until evenly combined.
3 Pour the mixture into the tin and arrange the prunes over the top. Sprinkle over any remaining brandy and bake for about 30 minutes until just firm. Serve with cream or crème fraîche.

PER SERVING 311 kcals, protein 5g, carbs 51g, fat 10g, sat fat 6g, fibre 3g, added sugar 31g, salt 0.18g

Mocha fudge cake with coffee icing

It's big, it's rich, it's moist – and impossible to resist.

TAKES 1 HOUR 5 MINUTES, PLUS 4 HOURS CHILLING • SERVES 10

FOR THE ICING
175g/6oz dark chocolate, melted
50g/2oz unsalted butter, melted
150ml/¼ pint double-strength espresso
1 tsp vanilla extract
300g/10oz icing sugar

FOR THE CAKE
300g/10oz plain flour, plus extra
2 tsp baking powder
1 tsp vanilla extract
3 eggs, separated
125ml/4fl oz milk
4 tbsp instant coffee granules
85g/3oz unsalted butter
300g/10oz caster sugar
85g/3oz dark chocolate, melted
125ml/4fl oz soured cream

1 Whisk together the cooled icing ingredients. Cover and chill for 3–4 hours.
2 Heat the oven to 180C/160C fan/gas 4. Butter and flour two 20cm/8in cake tins. Sift the flour and baking powder. Stir the vanilla into the egg yolks. Heat half the milk to boiling point, stir in the coffee to dissolve, then add the rest of the milk and cool.
3 Cream the butter and 200g/7oz of the caster sugar. Slowly whisk in the egg yolk mixture, then the melted chocolate. Fold in the sifted dry ingredients, the cooled milk and the soured cream. Whisk the egg whites until stiff; whisk in the remaining sugar to form firm peaks. Fold the egg whites into the cake mixture and pour into the tins. Bake for 30 minutes until risen. Cool, split each cake in two, and layer and coat with the icing.

PER SERVING 627 kcals, protein 8g, carbs 103g, fat 23g, sat fat 13g, fibre 2g, added sugar 77g, salt 0.42g

Sticky ginger cake with ginger fudge icing

You can make the cake a couple of days in advance, wrap well, then ice on the day of serving.

TAKES 1 HOUR 10 MINUTES • SERVES 16

200g/7oz unsalted butter, diced
175g/6oz molasses sugar
3 tbsp black treacle
150ml/¼ pint milk
2 large eggs, beaten
4 pieces stem ginger, drained from their syrup, chopped
300g/10oz self-raising flour
1 tbsp ground ginger

FOR THE ICING
4 tbsp ginger syrup, drained from jar
300g/10oz golden icing sugar, sifted
140g/5oz unsalted butter, softened
2 tsp lemon juice

1 Heat the oven to 160C/140C fan/gas 3. Butter and line the base of a 23cm/9in round cake tin. Gently melt the butter, sugar and treacle; cool briefly, then stir in the milk. Beat in the eggs and add the chopped stem ginger. Sift the flour, ground ginger and a pinch of salt into the warm mixture. Combine thoroughly.
2 Spoon the cake mixture into the tin and level the surface. Bake for 30–35 minutes or until firm and risen. Cool in the tin for an hour, then transfer to a wire rack.
3 Skewer the top of the cooled cake all over, then pour 2 tablespoons of the syrup over. Beat together the icing sugar, butter, lemon juice and the remaining ginger syrup, and spread over the cake.

PER SERVING 379 kcals, protein 3g, carbs 53g, fat 19g, sat fat 11g, fibre 1g, added sugar 37g, salt 0.27g

Mocha fudge cake with coffee icing

Sticky ginger cake with ginger fudge icing

Almond and chocolate torte with apricot cream

A special treat for dessert or at teatime.

TAKES 1 HOUR 5 MINUTES • SERVES 8–12

5 egg whites
200g/7oz golden caster sugar
100g/3½oz ground almonds
50g/2oz toasted flaked almonds
50g/2oz dark chocolate, chopped
FOR THE APRICOT CREAM
425ml/¾ pint double cream
300g/12oz apricot compote
FOR THE DECORATION
3 tbsp toasted flaked almonds
25g/1oz dark chocolate, shaved
icing sugar, for dusting

1 Heat the oven to 180C/160C fan/gas 4. Butter and line the base of a deep 25cm/10in cake tin. Whisk the egg whites until stiff, then gradually whisk in the golden caster sugar, a tablespoonful at a time.

2 Lightly fold in the ground almonds, the toasted flaked almonds and the chopped chocolate. Pour the mixture into the cake tin and bake for 40–45 minutes until crisp on top and light golden. Allow to cool in the tin for 5 minutes, then turn out and leave to cool on a wire rack.

3 Whip the cream until it just holds its shape. Spoon in the apricot compote, then fold it in gently to give you swirls of apricot. Spoon over the torte and scatter with toasted flaked almonds and chocolate shavings. Dust lightly with sifted icing sugar.

PER SERVING (for eight) 574 kcals, protein 9g, carbs 44g, fat 42g, sat fat 18g, fibre 3g, added sugar 37g, salt 0.16g

Pear, hazelnut and chocolate cake

Moist and fruity enough to serve warm with cream for pud, but just as good cold.

TAKES 1½ HOURS • SERVES 8

100g/3½oz blanched hazelnuts
140g/5oz self-raising flour
175g/6oz butter, cut into small pieces
140g/5oz golden caster sugar
2 large eggs, beaten
5 small ripe Conference pears
50g/2oz dark chocolate, chopped into small chunks
2 tbsp apricot jam

1 Heat the oven to 160C/140C fan/gas 3. Butter and line the base of a 20cm/8in round cake tin. Grind the hazelnuts in a food processor until fairly fine. Add the flour and mix briefly. Add the butter and pulse until it forms crumbs. Add the sugar and eggs, and mix briefly. Peel, core and chop two of the pears. Stir the pears and chocolate lightly into the cake mixture.

2 Spoon the mixture into the prepared tin and smooth the top. Peel, core and slice the remaining pears and scatter over the top of the cake. Press down lightly and bake for 50–60 minutes, until firm to the touch. Cool in the tin for 10 minutes, then turn out and cool on a wire rack. Warm the jam and brush over the top. Serve warm or cold.

PER SERVING 470 kcals, protein 6g, carbs 47g, fat 30g, sat fat 14g, fibre 3g, added sugar 18g, salt 0.5g

Almond and chocolate torte with apricot cream

Pear, hazelnut and chocolate cake

Dark chocolate and orange cake

Chocolate and orange is a classic combination.

TAKES 2 HOURS 10 MINUTES, PLUS 1½ HOURS COOLING TIME • SERVES 10

1 Seville orange
3 eggs
300g/10oz caster sugar
240ml/8½fl oz sunflower oil
100g/3½oz dark chocolate, broken into pieces
    and melted
25g/1oz cocoa powder
250g/9oz plain flour
1½ tsp baking powder
FOR THE CHOCOLATE GANACHE
200g/7oz dark chocolate, broken into pieces
225ml/8fl oz double cream
candied orange zest, to decorate

1 Pierce the orange with a skewer. Cook in a pan of boiling water for 30 minutes. Remove and whizz the whole orange in a food processor. Discard any pips and cool.
2 Heat the oven to 180C/160C fan/gas 4. Butter and line the base of a 23cm/9in round cake tin. Lightly beat the eggs, sugar and oil. Gradually beat in the puréed orange and cooled, melted chocolate. Sift in the cocoa, flour and baking powder. Mix well and pour into the tin. Bake for 55–60 minutes. Cool for 10 minutes, then turn out on to a wire rack.
3 Put the ganache chocolate into a heatproof bowl. Boil the cream in a pan, pour over the chocolate, and stir until smooth. Cool, up to 1½ hours, until firm but still spreadable. Spread over the cake, and decorate with the candied zest.

PER SERVING 703 kcals, protein 7g, carbs 73g, fat 45g, sat fat 16g, fibre 2g, added sugar 51g, salt 0.42g

Pecan ginger cake

Stays soft and moist in the middle, and the icing sets to a crisp meringue-like coating.

TAKES 1 HOUR • SERVES 10

200g/7oz self-raising flour
4 tsp ground ginger
1 tsp baking powder
½ tsp salt
200g/7oz butter
350g/12oz golden syrup
100g/3½oz light muscovado sugar
4 eggs, beaten
100g/3½oz pecan nuts, roughly chopped
100g/3½oz crystallised ginger, chopped
FOR THE TOPPING AND DECORATION
175g/6oz golden granulated sugar
1 egg white
pinch of cream of tartar
85g/3oz sugar
100g/3½oz pecan nut halves

1 Heat the oven to 180C/160C fan/gas 4. Butter and line the base of two 20cm/8in cake tins. Sift together the flour, ginger, baking powder and salt. Rub in the butter until it resembles crumbs.
2 Beat in the syrup, sugar, eggs, pecans and ginger. Pour into the tins and bake for 45 minutes until firm. Cool in the tins for 10 minutes, then turn out on to a wire rack.
3 Put the golden sugar, egg white, cream of tartar and 2 tablespoons hot water in a bowl set over (not in) a pan of simmering water. Beat for 10 minutes. Layer the cakes with a little icing; swirl the rest over the top and sides.
4 Heat the sugar with 4 tablespoons water until dissolved, then boil until it forms a caramel. Stir in the pecan halves, cool on an oiled baking sheet, then use to decorate.

PER SERVING 659 kcals, protein 7g, carbs 90g, fat 33g, sat fat 11g, fibre 2g, added sugar 43g, salt 1.3g

Pecan ginger cake

Dark chocolate and orange cake

Seriously rich chocolate cake

Made with ground almonds and dark chocolate, this flourless cake is beautifully rich and moist.

TAKES 55 MINUTES • SERVES 8–10

100g/3½oz butter, diced
140g/5oz best-quality dark chocolate, broken into pieces
6 eggs, separated
140g/5oz ground almonds
1 tbsp kirsch or Cointreau (optional)
85g/3oz caster sugar
cocoa powder, for dusting
crème fraîche, to serve

1 Heat the oven to 170C/150C fan/gas 3. Butter and line the base of a 23cm/9in springform cake tin. Dust the sides with a little flour. Melt the butter and chocolate, stir until smooth, and leave for about 5 minutes to cool slightly. Stir in the egg yolks, ground almonds, and the liqueur, if using.
2 Put the egg whites into a bowl, add a pinch of salt and whisk until soft peaks form. Continue whisking, sprinkling in the sugar a little at a time, until stiff peaks form. Stir 2 tablespoons of the whites into the chocolate mixture, then carefully fold in the remainder.
3 Spoon the mixture into the prepared tin and bake for 30–35 minutes until well risen and just firm. Cool in the tin. Remove the cake and peel away the paper. Dust with cocoa powder, slice, and serve with crème fraîche.

PER SERVING (for eight) 401 kcals, protein 10g, carbs 24g, fat 30g, sat fat 11g, fibre 2g, added sugar 22g, salt 0.66g

Chocca mocca caramel cake

Scatter over a handful of little chocolate eggs for an Easter treat.

TAKES 1½ HOURS • SERVES 10–12

2 tsp instant coffee granules/powder
2 tbsp cocoa
175g/6oz butter, softened
175g/6oz golden caster sugar
2 eggs
2 tbsp golden syrup
200g/7oz self-raising flour
4 tbsp milk
2 x 50g chocolate caramel bars, broken into pieces
FOR THE ICING
2 x 50g chocolate caramel bars, broken into pieces
50g/2oz butter
2 tbsp milk
100g/3½oz icing sugar, sifted

1 Heat the oven to 180C/160C fan/gas 4. Butter and line the base of a 20cm/8in round cake tin. Mix the coffee, cocoa and 2 tablespoons hot water to a smooth paste. Put the butter, sugar, eggs, syrup, flour, milk and cocoa paste in a bowl and beat for 2–3 minutes until smooth. Stir the caramel bar pieces into the mixture.
2 Turn the mixture into the prepared tin and smooth. Bake for 50–60 minutes, until the top springs back when you press it lightly. Cool in the tin for 5 minutes, then turn out, peel off the lining paper and leave to cool.
3 For the icing, gently heat the caramel bar pieces, butter and milk until smooth, stirring all the time, then remove from the heat and stir in the icing sugar. Leave to cool. Spread the icing over the top of the cooled cake.

PER SERVING (for ten) 474 kcals, protein 5g, carbs 59g, fat 26g, sat fat 15g, fibre 1g, added sugar 43g, salt 0.8g

Seriously rich chocolate cake

Chocca mocca caramel cake

Pumpkin and ginger teabread, page 65

Loaf cakes, teabreads and traybakes

Lamingtons

An Australian speciality, Lamingtons will delight the tastebuds with their combination of chocolate, vanilla cream and coconut.

TAKES 1½ HOURS, PLUS COOLING AND SETTING • MAKES 16

oil, for greasing
6 large eggs
140g/5oz golden caster sugar
200g/7oz self-raising flour
25g/1oz butter, melted
FOR THE VANILLA CREAM
250g/9oz icing sugar, sifted
1 tsp vanilla extract
50g/2oz butter, softened
2 tsp milk
FOR THE ICING
300g/10oz icing sugar
4 tbsp cocoa powder
25g/1oz butter
125ml/4fl oz milk
140g/5oz desiccated coconut

1 Heat the oven to 180C/160C fan/gas 4. Grease a 23cm-square cake tin. Beat the eggs and sugar until pale and thick. Fold in the flour, butter and 5 tablespoons of hot water. Pour into the tin and bake for 35 minutes until firm. Turn out on to a wire rack and cool.
2 Whip the vanilla-cream ingredients together until very thick and creamy. Cut the cake into 16, then slice each square horizontally in half and sandwich together with the cream.
3 Sift the sugar and cocoa for the icing into a bowl. Microwave the butter and milk on High for 1 minute (or in a pan on a low heat) until the butter has melted. Stir into the sugar mixture, spoon over each square and lift with a fork so the icing drains off. Put on a wire rack and sprinkle with the coconut. Leave to set.

PER SQUARE 360 kcals, protein 4.8g, carbs 57g, fat 14g, sat fat 9g, fibre 2g, sugar 46g, salt 0.33g

Swirly lemon drizzle fingers

Polenta (sometimes called fine cornmeal) gives these cakes their yellow colour and soft texture. If you'd rather, use a total of 200g/7oz self-raising flour instead.

TAKES 55 MINUTES, PLUS COOLING • MAKES 18

200g/7oz butter, well softened, plus extra for greasing
200g/7oz golden caster sugar
4 large eggs
100g/3½oz fine polenta or fine cornmeal
140g/5oz self-raising flour
zest 3 lemons
FOR THE SWIRL AND DRIZZLE
4 tbsp lemon curd
5 tbsp golden or white caster sugar
zest and juice 1 lemon

1 Heat the oven to 180C/160C fan/gas 4. Butter then line a rectangular baking tin or small roasting tin, about 20x30cm, with baking parchment.
2 Put the cake ingredients and a pinch of salt into a large bowl, then beat until creamy and smooth. Scoop into the tin, then level the top. Spoon the lemon curd over the batter in thick stripes then swirl into the cake – not too much or you won't see them once cooked. Bake for 35 minutes or until golden and risen. Don't open the oven before 30 minutes' cooking is up. Leave the cake in the tin for 10 minutes or until just cool enough to handle. Carefully transfer to a wire cooling rack.
3 For the drizzle, mix 4 tablespoons of the sugar with the lemon juice and spoon it over the warm cake. Toss the lemon zest with the remaining sugar and sprinkle over the top. Cut into fingers when cool.

PER FINGER 214 kcals, protein 3g, carbs 27g, fat 11g, sat fat 6g, fibre none, sugar 17g, salt 0.3g

Lamingtons

Swirly lemon drizzle fingers

Banana and walnut tea loaf

Sealed in a plastic food bag, this loaf will freeze for up to 3 months.

TAKES 1¼ HOURS • SERVES 12

100g/3½oz butter, softened
140g/5oz light muscovado sugar
2 eggs, lightly beaten
100g/3½oz walnuts, chopped
2 ripe bananas, mashed
2 tbsp milk
225g/8oz self-raising flour

1 Heat the oven to 180C/160C fan/gas 4. Butter and line a 1kg/2lb loaf tin. Cream the butter and sugar, then add the eggs. Set aside 25g/1oz walnuts, then fold the rest into the creamed mixture with the bananas and milk. Fold in the flour. Spoon into the tin and sprinkle over the reserved walnuts.
2 Bake for 55–60 minutes until risen. Stand for 10 minutes, then turn out, remove the lining paper and cool.

PER SERVING 267 kcals, protein 4g, carbs 33g, fat 14g, sat fat 5g, fibre 1g, added sugar 12g, salt 0.37g

Lemon and violet drizzle cake

This all-in-one cake mixes easily, keeps for a week wrapped in foil, and freezes well.

TAKES 1 HOUR • SERVES 15

100g/3½oz butter, softened
175g/6oz self-raising flour
1 tsp baking powder
175g/6oz golden caster sugar
2 large eggs
6 tbsp milk
finely grated rind 1 large lemon
FOR THE ICING AND DECORATION
juice 1 large lemon (you need 3 tablespoons)
100g/3½oz golden caster sugar
crystallized violets and mimosa balls (or yellow sugar balls), to decorate

1 Heat the oven to 180C/160C fan/gas 4. Butter and line the base of a shallow oblong tin (about 18 x 28cm/7 x 11in) with baking paper. Tip all the cake ingredients into a large mixing bowl and beat for 2–3 minutes, until the mixture drops easily off the spoon.
2 Spoon the mixture into the prepared tin and smooth the surface with the back of a spoon. Bake for 30–40 minutes, until golden and firm to the touch. Meanwhile, make the icing: beat together the lemon juice and sugar, pour the mixture evenly over the cake while it is still hot, then leave to cool.
3 Cut the cake into 15 squares. Top each one with a crystallised violet and mimosa ball.

PER SQUARE 175 kcals, protein 2g, carbs 29g, fat 7g, sat fat 4g, fibre none, added sugar 19g, salt 0.3g

Lemon and violet drizzle cake

Banana and walnut tea loaf

Coconut carrot slices

If you're looking for a treat for afternoon tea, or something to make for a cake sale, try this crunchy-topped traybake.

TAKES 50 MINUTES, PLUS COOLING • MAKES ABOUT 15

250g pack unsalted butter, plus extra for
    greasing
300g/10oz light muscovado sugar
1 tsp vanilla extract
3 large eggs
200g/7oz self-raising flour
50g/2oz desiccated coconut
200g/7oz carrot, grated
2 tsp ground mixed spice
FOR THE TOPPING
85g/3oz desiccated coconut
25g/1oz light muscovado sugar
25g/1oz melted butter

1 Butter and line a traybake or small roasting tin, about 20x30cm. Heat the oven to 180C/160C fan/gas 4. Gently melt the butter in a large pan, cool for 5 minutes, add the sugar, vanilla and eggs, then beat until smooth with a wooden spoon. Stir in the flour, coconut, carrot, spice and ¼ teaspoon salt.

2 Tip the mix into the tin, then bake for 30 minutes. Meanwhile, evenly mix the coconut and sugar for the topping, then stir in the melted butter. Smooth this over the cake, then bake for 10 minutes more until golden and a skewer inserted into the centre comes out clean. Cool, then cut into about 15 slices.

PER SLICE 347 kcals, protein 4g, carbs 35g, fat 22g, sat fat 15g, fibre 2g, sugar 25g, salt 0.22g

Better-for-you chocolate brownies

One classic brownie contains 314 kcals and 19g fat, but these feel-good treats have only 191 kcals and 11g fat.

TAKES 55 MINUTES, PLUS COOLING • MAKES 12

oil, for greasing
85g/3oz plain flour
25g/1oz cocoa powder
½ tsp bicarbonate of soda
100g/3½oz golden caster sugar
50g/2oz light muscovado sugar
85g/3oz dark chocolate, 70% cocoa solids,
    melted then cooled
½ tsp coffee granules
1 tsp vanilla extract
2 tbsp buttermilk
1 large egg, beaten
100g/3½oz mayonnaise

1 Heat the oven to 180C/160C fan/gas 4. Lightly oil and line the base of a 19cm-square cake tin. Combine the flour, cocoa and bicarbonate of soda. Stir both the sugars into the cooled chocolate with the coffee, vanilla and buttermilk. Stir in 1 tablespoon warm water. Beat in the egg, then stir in the mayonnaise just until smooth and glossy. Sift over the flour and cocoa mix, then gently fold in with a spatula.

2 Spread the mix evenly into the tin. Bake for 30 minutes. When a skewer is inserted into the middle, it should come out with just a few moist crumbs sticking to it. Leave in the tin until completely cold, then loosen the sides with a round-bladed knife. Turn out on to a board, peel off the lining paper and cut into 12 squares.

PER BROWNIE 191 kcals, protein 2g, carbs 23g, fat 11g, sat fat 3g, fibre 1g, sugar 16g, salt 0.28g

Blackberry and apple loaf

Try other fruits when in season – raspberries and tayberries would be good.

TAKES 2 HOURS • SERVES 10

250g/9oz self-raising flour
175g/6oz butter
175g/6oz light muscovado sugar
½ tsp ground cinnamon
2 rounded tbsp demerara sugar
1 small eating apple, unpeeled, coarsely
    grated down to the core
2 large eggs, beaten
finely grated zest 1 orange
1 tsp baking powder
225g/8oz blackberries

1 Heat the oven to 180C/160C fan/gas 4. Butter and line the base of a 1kg/2lb loaf tin. Rub the flour, butter and muscovado sugar together to make fine crumbs. Reserve 5 tablespoons of this mixture for the topping, and mix into it the cinnamon and demerara sugar. Set aside.
2 Mix the apple in with the eggs and the zest. Stir the baking powder into the rubbed-in mixture, then quickly and lightly stir in the egg mixture. Don't overmix.
3 Gently fold in three quarters of the berries. Spoon into the tin and level. Scatter the rest of the berries on top. Sprinkle over the topping and bake for 1 hour 20 minutes, testing with a skewer. After 50 minutes, cover loosely with foil. Leave in the tin for 30 minutes, then cool on a wire rack.

PER SERVING 327 kcals, protein 4g, carbs 44g, fat 16g, sat fat 10g, fibre 2g, added sugar 23g, salt 0.77g

Gooseberry and almond streusel squares

Make the most of the short gooseberry season with these scrumptious squares. If you're too late, though, frozen berries work well too.

TAKES 1 HOUR 5 MINUTES–1¼ HOURS, PLUS COOLING • MAKES ABOUT 8

250g/9oz chilled butter, chopped
250g/9oz self-raising flour
125g/4oz ground almonds
125g/4oz light muscovado sugar
350g/12oz gooseberries, fresh or frozen
85g/3oz caster sugar, plus extra to sprinkle
50g/2oz flaked almonds

1 Heat the oven to 190C/170C fan/gas 5. Line a 27x18cm baking tin with baking parchment. Rub the butter into the flour, almonds and sugar to make crumbs, then firmly press two-thirds of the mixture on to the base and sides of the tin. Toss the gooseberries with the caster sugar, then scatter over the top.
2 Mix the flaked almonds into the remaining crumbs, then scatter over the gooseberries. Bake for 50 minutes–1 hour until golden and the fruit is bubbling a little around the edges. Dredge with more caster sugar, then cool in the tin. Serve cut into about eight squares.

PER SQUARE 589 kcals, protein 8g, carbs 56g, fat 38g, sat fat 17g, fibre 4g, sugar 32g, salt 0.78g

Blackcurrant crumble squares

These moist but crumbly squares are best eaten on the day, but will freeze for up to 3 months.

TAKES 1 HOUR • MAKES 12

115g/4oz butter, softened
175g/6oz caster sugar
1 egg
300g/10oz self-raising flour
125ml/4fl oz milk
200g//oz fresh blackcurrants, destalked
FOR THE CRUMBLE
115g/4oz caster sugar
85g/3oz plain flour
finely grated rind 1 lemon
50g/2oz butter

1 Heat the oven to 180C/160C fan/gas 4. Butter a 28 x 18cm/12 x 7in oblong cake tin and line with baking paper. (You could also use a 23cm/9in square tin or a 25cm/10in round tin.)
2 Beat the butter and sugar in a large bowl with an electric hand whisk until the mixture is pale and fluffy. Whisk in the egg, then carefully fold in the flour and milk until thoroughly combined. Spoon into the tin and spread evenly. Sprinkle over the blackcurrants.
3 Mix together the sugar, flour and lemon rind. Rub in the butter until the mixture is crumbly, then sprinkle on top of the squares. Bake for 45 minutes until the topping is golden and the blackcurrants start to burst through; leave to cool in the tin. When cool, lift the cake out, and cut into squares.

PER SQUARE 315 kcals, protein 4g, carbs 50g, fat 13g, sat fat 8g, fibre 2g, added sugar 25g, salt 0.29g

Apricot crumb squares

Ideal with a cup of tea at home, or to enjoy at your next picnic.

TAKES 1¼ HOURS • MAKES 16

FOR THE TOPPING
175g/6oz plain flour
140g/5oz light muscovado sugar
140g/5oz butter, softened
1 tsp ground cinnamon
½ tsp salt
FOR THE CAKE
175g/6oz butter, softened
200g/7oz golden caster sugar
3 large eggs
175g/6oz plain flour
1 tsp baking powder
2–3 tbsp milk
8 fresh apricots (or canned in natural juice), quartered
icing sugar, for dusting

1 Heat oven to 180C/160C fan/gas 4, and butter a shallow 23cm/9in square cake tin. Put the five topping ingredients in a food processor and blend to make a sticky crumble.
2 In a separate bowl, blend the butter, sugar, eggs, flour and baking powder using an electric hand whisk or wooden spoon, gradually adding enough milk to make a creamy mixture that drops from a spoon. Spread in the tin and scatter with apricots. Top with the crumble and press down.
3 Bake for 45–50 minutes until golden and a skewer inserted into the centre comes out clean. Cool in the tin, cut into 16 squares and dust with icing sugar.

PER SQUARE 332 kcals, protein 4g, carbs 42g, fat 18g, sat fat 11g, fibre 1g, added sugar 22g, salt 0.52g

Blackcurrant crumble squares

Apricot crumb squares

Autumn plum crunch cake

Moist and moreish, this rich cake has the most wonderful, crunchy sugarplum topping.

TAKES 1½ HOURS • SERVES 10

2 eggs, plus 1 egg yolk
140g/5oz butter, softened
140g/5oz golden caster sugar
140g/5oz self-raising flour
grated zest and juice 1 orange
200g/7oz plums, stoned, half roughly chopped
    into pieces and half cut into wedges

FOR THE TOPPING

1½ tbsp fresh lemon juice
200g/7oz golden caster sugar
25g/1oz rough sugar pieces (or sugar cubes),
    roughly crushed

1 Heat the oven to 160C/140C fan/gas 3. Butter and line the base of a 1kg/2lb loaf tin. Lightly beat the eggs and egg yolk with a pinch of salt.
2 Beat the butter and sugar in a bowl until light and fluffy. Pour in the eggs a little at a time, beating well after each addition. Fold in the flour with the orange zest and 2 tablespoons of the juice, then fold in the roughly chopped plums. Spoon into the prepared tin and scatter the plum wedges over. Bake for 50 minutes or until a skewer inserted into the centre comes out clean.
3 Cool for 10 minutes, then turn out on to a wire rack. Mix the remaining orange juice with the lemon juice and caster sugar. Spoon over the cooling cake and sprinkle with the crushed sugar pieces. Cool until set.

PER SERVING 327 kcals, protein 3g, carbs 51g, fat 14g, sat fat 8g, fibre 1g, added sugar 38g, salt 0.45g

Spotted dog

Made in a flash, this is best cut into thick slices and spread with butter while still warm.

TAKES 50 MINUTES • SERVES 10–12

300g/10oz plain flour
½ tsp salt
1 tsp bicarbonate of soda
3 tbsp caster sugar
100g/3½oz mixed dried fruit
1 egg, beaten
200ml/7fl oz buttermilk

1 Heat the oven to 190C/170C fan/gas 5. Butter a 1kg/2lb loaf tin. Sift the flour, salt and bicarbonate of soda into a mixing bowl. Stir in the sugar, make a well in the centre and add the dried fruit, egg and buttermilk. Mix lightly and quickly into the flour for a soft dough.
2 Using floured hands, remove the dough from the bowl and knead very briefly. Then press the dough into the prepared tin. Bake for 35–40 minutes until the top is a dark golden colour and the loaf feels firm to the touch. Turn out and leave to cool. Serve thickly sliced and buttered.

PER SERVING (for ten) 163 kcals, protein 4g, carbs 36g, fat 1g, sat fat 0.3g, fibre 1g, added sugar 5g, salt 0.66g

Spotted dog

Autumn plum crunch cake

Rhubarb spice cake

A wonderfully moist cake that is reminiscent of old-fashioned gingerbread. Serve it for tea or heat up a thick slice in the microwave and have it for pud with a dollop of custard.

TAKES 1 HOUR 10 MINUTES, PLUS COOLING • SERVES 12

140g/5oz butter, softened, plus extra for greasing
300g/10oz self-raising flour
2 tsp ground mixed spice
1 tsp ground ginger
100g/3½oz dark muscovado sugar
250g/9oz golden syrup
1 tsp bicarbonate of soda
2 large eggs, beaten
300g/10oz rhubarb, cut into short lengths
icing sugar, for dusting

1 Heat the oven to 180C/160C fan/gas 4 and put the kettle on. Butter and line a deep 20cm-square cake tin. Sift the flour and spices into a bowl. Beat together the butter and sugar until light and fluffy in a food processor, then beat in the golden syrup. Dissolve the bicarbonate of soda in 200ml/7fl oz boiling water, then gradually pour through the spout of the processor. Pulse in the flour mix, then add the eggs, mixing briefly. Remove the bowl from the processor, then gently stir in the rhubarb.
2 Pour the mixture into the tin and bake for 50 minutes–1 hour, until the cake feels firm to the touch and springs back when pressed. Cool in the tin for 5 minutes, then turn out and cool on a wire rack. Lightly dust with icing sugar.

PER SLICE 290 kcals, protein 4g, carbs 46g, fat 11g, sat fat 7g, fibre 1g, sugar 27g, salt 0.89g

Better-for-you carrot cake

A square of classic carrot cake contains 315 kcals and 20g fat (5g sat fat). This one contains 217 kcals and 9g fat (1g sat fat) – so now you really can have your cake and eat it!

TAKES 1½ HOURS, PLUS COOLING • SERVES 16

zest and juice 1 medium orange
140g/5oz raisins
125ml/4fl oz rapeseed oil, plus extra for greasing
115g/4oz self-raising flour
115g/4oz plain wholemeal flour
1 tsp baking powder, plus a pinch
1 tsp bicarbonate of soda
1 rounded tsp ground cinnamon
2 large eggs
140g/5oz dark muscovado sugar
300g/10oz finely grated carrot
FOR THE FROSTING
100g/3½oz light soft cheese, straight from the fridge
100g/3½oz Quark
3 tbsp icing sugar, sifted
½ tsp finely grated orange zest
1 tsp fresh lemon juice

1 Heat the oven to 160C/140C fan/gas 3. Mix the orange zest and 3 tablespoons of juice with the raisins. Oil then line the base of a deep 20cm-square cake tin. Mix the flours, baking powder, the bicarbonate of soda and cinnamon.
2 Separate one egg. Add the remaining whole egg to the yolk, then whisk in the sugar for 1–2 minutes until thick. Whisk in the oil. Fold in the flour mix in two goes. Whisk the egg white and pinch of bicarbonate of soda to soft peaks.
3 Fold the carrot, raisins and juice into the flour mixture. Fold in the whisked white, then pour into the tin. Bake for 1 hour until risen and firm or until a skewer inserted in to the centre comes out clean. Cool for 5 minutes in the tin, then on a wire rack.
4 For the frosting, beat everything together until smooth. Swirl over the cake before slicing.

PER SQUARE 217 kcals, protein 4g, carbs 31g, fat 9g, sat fat 1g, fibre 2g, sugar 21g, salt 0.52g

Rhubarb spice cake

Better-for-you carrot cake

Chocolate cinnamon crumb squares

These moist little squares are deliciously chocolatey without being sickly.

TAKES 2 HOURS • MAKES 16

FOR THE CRUMBLE TOPPING
50g/2oz plain flour
1 tbsp cocoa powder
2 tsp ground cinnamon
50g/2oz light muscovado sugar
50g/2oz butter, cut into pieces

FOR THE CAKE
200g/7oz dark chocolate, broken into pieces
175g/6oz butter, softened
200g/7oz light muscovado sugar
3 eggs
175g/6oz self-raising flour
icing sugar, for dusting

1 Heat the oven to 170C/150C fan/gas 3. Butter and line the base and sides of a 20cm/8in square cake tin. For the topping, put the flour, cocoa, cinnamon, sugar and the butter into a food processor, then pulse until the mixture forms a crumble. Set aside.

2 For the cake, put the chocolate in a bowl and melt in the microwave on Medium for 2–3 minutes. Put the butter, sugar, eggs and flour in a bowl and beat for 2–3 minutes, until well mixed. Stir in the chocolate until it is evenly mixed in.

3 Tip the mixture into the tin and smooth. Sprinkle the crumble evenly over the top. Bake for 50–60 minutes, until a skewer inserted into the centre comes out clean. Leave to cool for 10 minutes in the tin, then turn out to cool on a wire rack. Dust the top lightly with icing sugar.

PER SQUARE 298 kcals, protein 3g, carbs 36g, fat 16g, sat fat 10g, fibre 1g, added sugar 25g, salt 0.43g

Banana nut brownies

Deliciously moist, chocolatey and utterly irresistible – they'll keep for up to a week, tightly wrapped in foil.

TAKES 50 MINUTES • MAKES 15

175g/6oz butter, cut into pieces
300g/10oz light muscovado sugar
175g/6oz dark chocolate, broken into pieces
100g bag nuts, toasted and chopped
3 eggs, beaten
2 ripe bananas, mashed
100g/3½oz self-raising flour
2 tbsp cocoa powder
1 tsp baking powder

1 Heat the oven to 180C/160C fan/gas 4. Butter and line an 18 x 28cm/ 7 x 11in Swiss roll tin with baking paper. Put the butter, sugar and chocolate in a large pan and heat gently, stirring, until melted and smooth, then remove the pan from the heat.

2 Stir in the nuts, eggs and bananas until well mixed, then sift in the flour, cocoa and baking powder.

3 Pour the mixture into the tin and bake for 30 minutes until firm in the centre. Cool in the tin, then turn out and cut into 15 squares.

PER BROWNIE 336 kcals, protein 5g, carbs 37g, fat 20g, sat fat 9g, fibre 1g, added sugar 28g, salt 0.5g

Banana teabread

The natural sweetness provided by the bananas helps reduce the amount of sugar that needs to be used.

TAKES 1 HOUR 35 MINUTES • SERVES 10

175g/6oz plain wholemeal flour
50g/2oz medium oatmeal
100g/3½oz butter, softened
100g/3½oz dark muscovado sugar
2 tsp baking powder
¼ tsp ground cinnamon
2 eggs, beaten
3–4 ripe bananas, about 350g/12oz, peeled
    and mashed
100g/3½oz walnuts, roughly chopped

1 Heat the oven to 180C/160C fan/gas 4. Butter and line the base of a 1kg/2lb loaf tin with baking paper. Put the wholemeal flour, oatmeal, butter, sugar, baking powder, cinnamon and eggs into a large bowl and, using an electric hand whisk, beat together until evenly mixed. Stir in the bananas and walnuts, taking care not to overmix.
2 Spoon the mixture into the prepared tin and bake for 1¼ hours or until a skewer inserted into the centre comes out clean (cover the cake with foil halfway through cooking to prevent the top from overbrowning). Allow the cake to cool in the tin for 5 minutes, then carefully turn out, peel off the lining paper and cool completely on a wire rack.

PER SERVING 309 kcals, protein 6g, carbs 34g, fat 17g, sat fat 3g, fibre 3g, added sugar 10g, salt 0.53g

Peach and cherry teabread

Measuring the ingredients in a jug makes this really easy to throw together – though it does need to be started the day before baking.

TAKES 1¾ HOURS, PLUS OVERNIGHT SOAKING • SERVES 12–14

300ml/½ pint ready-to-eat dried peaches,
    chopped
150ml/¼ pint undyed glacé cherries, halved
150ml/¼ pint raisins
300ml/½ pint light muscovado sugar
300ml/½ pint freshly made hot tea
1 egg, beaten
1 pint self-raising flour
1 tsp ground cinnamon
icing sugar, for dusting

1 Put the fruit and sugar in a bowl, pour over the tea and stir well. Cover with a tea towel and leave overnight for the fruit to plump up.
2 Heat the oven to 160C/140C fan/gas 3. Butter and line the base of a 1kg/2lb loaf tin with greaseproof paper. Stir the egg into the steeped fruit mixture, then sift in the flour and cinnamon. Mix well, then turn into the prepared tin and smooth the top.
3 Bake for 1¼–1½ hours until the teabread is risen and golden. Test with a skewer (it should come out clean). Cool in the tin for 10 minutes, then turn out and cool on a wire rack. Dust the top with icing sugar.

PER SERVING (for twelve) 297 kcals, protein 4g, carbs 71g, fat 1g, sat fat 0.4g, fibre 3g, added sugar 31g, salt 0.31g

Mincemeat and marzipan teabread

A treat for tea by the fire, this afternoon bake keeps moist, well-wrapped, for 4–5 days.

TAKES 1 HOUR 20 MINUTES • SERVES 12

200g/7oz self-raising flour
100g/3½oz cold butter, cut into pieces
85g/3oz light muscovado sugar
85g/3oz marzipan, cut into 1cm/½in cubes
2 eggs
300g/10oz mincemeat
2 tbsp flaked almonds
icing sugar, for dusting (optional)

1 Heat the oven to 180C/160C fan/gas 4. Butter a 1kg/2lb loaf tin and line the base with greaseproof paper. Tip the flour into a bowl, add the cold butter and rub until the mixture forms fine crumbs. Stir in the sugar and marzipan cubes.
2 In another bowl, lightly whisk the eggs, then stir in the mincemeat. Stir this into the flour mixture until evenly combined. Spoon into the prepared loaf tin, smooth, and sprinkle the flaked almonds over the top. Bake for 1 hour until the teabread is risen and golden brown, or a skewer inserted into the centre comes out clean. Lightly dust the teabread with icing sugar, if using, while it is still hot.
3 Allow to cool in the tin for 10 minutes, then tip on to a wire rack to cool completely. Peel off the lining paper and cut into slices – it's also very good spread with butter.

PER SERVING 265 kcals, protein 4g, carbs 41g, fat 11g, sat fat 5g, fibre 1g, added sugar 15g, salt 0.44g

Walnut, date and honey cake

Choose a richly flavoured Greek or Mexican honey for an extra-special taste.

TAKES 1 HOUR 25 MINUTES • SERVES 8–10

225g/8oz self-raising flour
½ tsp ground cinnamon
175g/6oz butter, softened
100g/3½oz light muscovado sugar
3 tbsp clear honey
2 eggs, beaten
2 medium, ripe bananas, about 250g/9oz total weight in their skins
100g/3½oz stoned dates
50g pack walnut pieces

1 Heat the oven to 160C/140C fan/gas 3. Line the base and long sides of a 1kg/2lb loaf tin with baking parchment, thoroughly buttering the tin and paper. Tip the flour, cinnamon, butter, sugar, 2 tablespoons of the honey and the eggs into a large mixing bowl. Mash the bananas and chop the dates (kitchen scissors are easiest for this), and add to the bowl. Beat the mixture for 2–3 minutes, using a wooden spoon or hand-held mixer, until well blended.
2 Spoon into the prepared tin and smooth. Scatter the walnut pieces over the top. Bake for 1 hour, then lightly press the top – it should feel firm. If not, bake for a further 10 minutes.
3 Cool for 15 minutes, then lift out of the tin using the paper. When cold, drizzle the remaining honey over. Cut into thick slices.

PER SERVING (for eight) 440 kcals, protein 6g, carbs 54g, fat 24g, sat fat 13g, fibre 1.5g, added sugar 25g, salt 0.7g

Mincemeat and marzipan teabread

Walnut, date and honey cake

Cappuccino bars

These moreish bars can be frozen, unfrosted, for up to 2 months.

TAKES 50 MINUTES • MAKES 24

1 tsp cocoa powder, plus extra for dusting
2 rounded tbsp coffee granules
225g/8oz butter, softened
225g/8oz caster sugar
4 eggs
225g/8oz self-raising flour
1 tsp baking powder
FOR THE FROSTING
100g/3½oz white chocolate, broken into
    pieces
50g/2oz butter, softened
3 tbsp milk
175g/6oz icing sugar

1 Heat the oven to 180C/160C fan/gas 4. Butter and line the bottom of a shallow 28 x 18cm/11 x 7in oblong tin. Mix the cocoa and coffee granules into 2 tablespoons warm water. Put in a large bowl with the other cake ingredients.
2 Whisk for about 2 minutes with an electric hand blender to combine, then tip into the tin and level out. Bake for 35–40 minutes until risen and firm to the touch. Cool in the tin for 10 minutes, then cool on a rack. Peel off the paper.
3 For the frosting, melt the chocolate, butter and milk in a bowl over a pan of simmering water. Remove the bowl and sift in the icing sugar. Beat until smooth, then spread over the cake. Finish with a dusting of cocoa powder. Cut into 24 bars.

PER BAR 219 kcals, protein 3g, carbs 27g, fat 12g, sat fat 6g, fibre trace, added sugar 19g, salt 0.43g

Toffee brownies

Unrefined dark muscovado sugar gives these brownies a sticky toffee flavour.

TAKES 1 HOUR 5 MINUTES, PLUS 1 HOUR COOLING • MAKES 16

350g/12oz dark chocolate (preferably around
    50–60% cocoa solids), broken into pieces
250g/9oz unsalted butter, cut into pieces
3 large eggs
250g/9oz dark muscovado sugar
85g/3oz plain flour
1 tsp baking powder

1 Heat the oven to 160C/140C fan/gas 3. Butter and line the base of a shallow 23cm/9in square cake tin. Melt the chocolate and butter together, then stir well and cool.
2 Whisk the eggs until pale, then whisk in the sugar until thick and glossy and well combined. Gently fold in the melted-chocolate mixture, then sift in the flour and baking powder, and gently stir until smooth.
3 Pour into the prepared cake tin and bake for 30–35 minutes, or until firm to the touch. Test by inserting a wooden cocktail stick into the middle – there should be a few moist crumbs sticking to it. The mixture will still be soft in the centre, but will firm up on cooling.
4 Cool in the tin on a wire rack for at least 1 hour, then cut into 16 squares and finish cooling on the rack.

PER BROWNIE 324 kcals, protein 3g, carbs 34g, fat 20g, sat fat 12g, fibre 1g, added sugar 30g, salt 0.14g

Toffee brownies

Cappuccino bars

Peach melba squares

With juicy peach and raspberry in every bite, these squares are special enough for summer afternoon tea, or served warm as dessert with a scoop of ice cream.

TAKES 1 HOUR 20 MINUTES, PLUS COOLING • MAKES 12

250g pack unsalted butter, plus extra for
   greasing
300g/10oz golden caster sugar
1 tsp vanilla extract
3 large eggs
200g/7oz self-raising flour
50g/2oz ground almonds
2 just ripe peaches, stoned, halved, then
   each half cut into 3
100g/3½oz raspberries
handful of flaked almonds
1 tbsp icing sugar, to dust

1 Butter and line a traybake or small roasting tin, about 20x30cm. Heat the oven to 180C/160C fan/gas 4. Gently melt the butter in a large pan, cool for 5 minutes, add the sugar, vanilla and eggs, then beat until smooth with a wooden spoon. Stir in the flour, almonds and a pinch of salt.
2 Tip the mix into the tin, then lay the peach slices evenly on top – that way each square of cake will have a bite of fruit. Scatter the raspberries and almonds over, then bake for 1 hour–1 hour 10 minutes, covering with foil after 40 minutes. Test with a skewer; the middle should have just a tiny hint of squidginess, which will firm up once the cake cools. Cool in the tin for 20 minutes, then lift out on to a wire cooling rack. Once cold, dredge with icing sugar, then cut into squares.

PER SQUARE 385 kcals, protein 5g, carbs 43g, fat 23g, sat fat 12g, fibre 2g, sugar 31g, salt 0.22g

Chocolate and orange fudge squares

No need to buy chocolate with a high cocoa content for this recipe. Once melted with muscovado you'll have the fudgy, chocolatey flavour you need.

TAKES 40 MINUTES, PLUS COOLING • MAKES 15

175g/6oz butter, plus extra for greasing
200g/7oz dark chocolate, broken into cubes
200g/7oz dark muscovado sugar
3 large eggs, separated
140g/5oz plain flour
1 tsp vanilla extract
zest 1 orange
FOR THE TOPPING
200g tub soft cheese
½ tsp vanilla extract
50g/2oz icing sugar

1 Heat the oven to 180C/160C fan/gas 4. Butter and line a traybake tin, about 23 x 23cm. Put the chocolate, sugar and butter in a pan, then heat very gently for about 5 minutes, stirring every minute until the butter and chocolate have melted. Leave to cool for 10 minutes. Beat in the egg yolks, flour, vanilla and half the orange zest.
2 Put the egg whites into a very clean large bowl, then whisk until they stand up in peaks. Stir a spoonful of the whites into the chocolate mix to loosen it, then carefully fold in the rest with a metal spoon. Pour the mix into the tin, then bake for 25 minutes or until evenly risen and just firm to the touch. Cool in the tin, then cut into squares.
3 Beat together the cheese, vanilla, sugar and remaining orange zest until smooth. Spread over each chocolate square and serve.

PER SQUARE 289 kcals, protein 5g, carbs 34g, fat 16g, sat fat 9g, fibre 1g, sugar 27g, salt 0.37g

Peach melba squares

Chocolate and orange fudge squares

Sticky marmalade tealoaf

Use a chunky marmalade to give this loaf extra texture and a pretty top.

TAKES 1½ HOURS • SERVES 12

140g/5oz marmalade (about ⅓ of
  a 454g jar)
175g/6oz butter, softened
175g/6oz light muscovado sugar
3 eggs, beaten
225g/8oz self-raising flour
½ tsp baking powder
2 tsp ground ginger
1 tsp mixed spice
100g packet pecan nut halves

1 Heat the oven to 180C/160C fan/gas 4. Butter a 1kg/2lb loaf tin and line with greaseproof paper. Set aside 1 tablespoon of the marmalade in a small pan. In a bowl, blend the remaining marmalade, butter, sugar, eggs, flour, baking powder and spices for 1–2 minutes until smooth and light. Stir in about three quarters of the pecan nut halves.
2 Tip into the prepared tin and smooth the top. Sprinkle with the reserved pecans. Bake for about 1–1¼ hours until a skewer inserted into the centre comes out clean. Cover loosely with foil after 40 minutes. Once cooked, carefully remove from the tin, and cool slightly on a wire rack.
3 Gently heat the reserved marmalade, stirring until it's smooth, and spread the glaze over the top of the warm loaf. Serve in slices.

PER SERVING 339 kcals, protein 4g, carbs 40g, fat 20g, sat fat 8g, fibre 1g, added sugar 24g, salt 0.56g

Date and walnut tea loaf

Although a fast and easy recipe for tea, this loaf is best made a day or two in advance.

TAKES 1 HOUR 40 MINUTES, PLUS COOLING TIME • SERVES 10–12

200g/7oz stoned dates, chopped
1 tsp bicarbonate of soda
100g/3½oz butter, cut into pieces
300g/10oz self-raising flour, sifted
50g/2oz chopped walnuts
100g/3½oz dark muscovado sugar
1 egg, beaten
2 tbsp demerara sugar

1 Mix the dates and bicarbonate of soda in a large bowl with a pinch of salt. Pour in 300ml/ ½ pint hot water, stir well and leave until cold. Heat the oven to 180C/160C fan/gas 4. Butter a 1kg/2lb loaf tin and line the base and two long sides.
2 Rub the butter pieces into the flour until the mixture resembles coarse breadcrumbs. Stir in the walnuts and muscovado sugar until evenly combined.
3 Tip the flour mixture and the egg into the cooled dates. Beat well to mix, then pour into the prepared tin and sprinkle the demerara sugar on top. Bake in the oven for 1–1¼ hours or until a skewer inserted into the centre comes out clean. Cool in the tin for 5 minutes, then turn it out on to a wire rack. Double-wrap the cooled cake, and store in an airtight tin for 1–2 days before eating.

PER SERVING (for ten) 317 kcals, protein 5g, carbs 49g, fat 13g, sat fat 6g, fibre 2g, added sugar 14g, salt 0.9g

Pumpkin and ginger teabread

The pumpkin adds a depth of flavour, a certain sweetness and a lusciously moist texture.

TAKES 1½ HOURS • SERVES 10

175g/6oz butter, melted
140g/5oz clear honey
1 large egg, beaten
250g/9oz raw peeled pumpkin or butternut
    squash, coarsely grated (about 500g/1lb 2oz
    before peeling and seeding)
100g/3½oz light muscovado sugar
350g/12oz self-raising flour
1 tbsp ground ginger
2 tbsp demerara sugar, plus extra for sprinkling
    (optional)

1 Heat the oven to 180C/160C fan/gas 4. Butter and line the base and two long sides of a 1kg/2lb loaf tin with a strip of baking paper.
2 Mix the butter, honey and egg, and stir in the pumpkin or squash. Then mix in the sugar, flour and ginger.
3 Pour into the prepared tin and sprinkle the top with the demerara sugar. Bake for 50–60 minutes, until risen and golden brown. Leave in the tin for 5 minutes, then turn out and cool on a wire rack. Sprinkle more demerara sugar over the warm cake, if you wish. Serve thickly sliced and buttered.

PER SERVING 351 kcals, protein 4g, carbs 52g, fat 15g, sat fat 9g, fibre 1g, added sugar 24g, salt 0.69g

Triple ginger and spice cake

If you're looking for a slice with spice, try this deliciously moist ginger cake. If you can resist cutting it, the cake is best eaten a day or two after baking, when it gets even stickier.

TAKES 1 HOUR 20 MINUTES, PLUS COOLING • MAKES 16

250g pack butter
250g/9oz dark muscovado sugar
250g/9oz black treacle
300ml/10fl oz milk
2 large eggs
100g/3½oz stem ginger in syrup, finely chopped
375g/13oz plain flour
2 tsp bicarbonate of soda
1 tsp ground allspice
2 tsp ground ginger
FOR THE ICING
3 tbsp ginger syrup from the jar
5 tbsp icing sugar, sifted

1 Butter and line a 23cm-square baking tin (or use a shallow roasting tin, about 30x20cm). Heat the oven to 160C/140C fan/gas 3. Gently melt together the butter, sugar and treacle in a pan. Take off the heat then stir in the milk. Beat in the eggs.
2 Mix the chopped ginger and dry ingredients in a large bowl, and make a well in the centre. Pour in the melted mix then stir to a smooth batter. Pour into the tin, then bake for 1 hour until risen and firm and a skewer inserted into the centre comes out clean. Resist taking a peek beforehand as this cake can easily sink. Cool in the tin, then ice (or wrap well and keep in a cool, dry place for up to a week).
3 Stir together the syrup and icing sugar to make the icing and drizzle over. Cut into 16 squares.

PER SQUARE 360 kcals, protein 4g, carbs 57g, fat 14g, sat fat 9g, fibre none, sugar 39g, salt 0.81g

Starry toffee cake squares

These cakes are truly scrumptious and so simple to whip together.

TAKES 1½ HOURS • MAKES 24

200g/7oz butter
200g/7oz golden syrup
300g/10oz self-raising flour
1 tsp salt
200g/7oz light muscovado sugar
3 eggs
2 tbsp milk
225g/8oz yellow marzipan
red and green food colouring
icing sugar, for dusting

1 Heat the oven to 160C/140C fan/gas 3. Butter and line the base of a 32 x 23 x 2cm/13 x 9 x 1in Swiss roll tin. Gently melt the butter and syrup in a pan, stirring to combine. Cool for 15 minutes.
2 Sift the flour with the salt and stir in the muscovado sugar. Beat in the cooled syrup mixture. Beat the eggs and milk, and combine with the flour mixture until smooth. Pour into the tin and level with a spoon. Bake for 40–50 minutes until risen and firm in the centre. Leave in the tin to cool for 10 minutes. Tip on to a wire rack until cold.
3 Divide the marzipan into three; colour one piece with red and another with green colouring. Roll out and cut out star shapes. Cut the cake into 24 squares, top with marzipan stars and dust with icing sugar.

PER SQUARE 217 kcals, protein 3g, carbs 34g, fat 9g, sat fat 5g, fibre 1g, added sugar 22g, salt 0.37g

Chocolate brownie chunks with chocolate dip

For an even more delicious treat, pop these tiny temptations into a low oven to warm through quickly before serving.

TAKES 45 MINUTES, PLUS COOLING • SERVES 8

200g/7oz dark chocolate, broken into chunks
100g/3½oz milk chocolate, broken into chunks
85g/3oz butter
100g/3½oz light muscovado sugar
85g/3oz dark muscovado sugar
3 large eggs, at room temperature and lightly beaten
140g/5oz plain flour
140g/5oz walnuts, roughly chopped
200g/7oz natural yogurt

1 Heat the oven to 180C/160C fan/gas 4 and line the base of a shallow 20cm-square baking tin with baking parchment. Melt 100g of the dark chocolate, all of the milk chocolate and the butter in a heatproof bowl over a pan of simmering water. Stir in the sugars off the heat. Cool for a little while you prepare the rest of the ingredients.
2 Stir the eggs into the chocolate mixture, followed by the flour, walnuts and a pinch of salt until really well combined. Pour the mixture into the prepared tin, then bake for 25–30 minutes until a skewer inserted into the centre of the cake comes out with sticky crumbs. Cool in the tin.
3 For the dip, gently melt the remaining dark chocolate as above, then stir into the yogurt and chill. To serve, cut the brownies into chunks, then spoon the dip into small bowls to serve alongside.

PER CHUNK 588 kcals, protein 11g, carbs 63g, fat 35g, sat fat 14g, fibre 2g, sugar 49g, salt 0.34g

Starry toffee cake squares

Chocolate brownie chunks with chocolate dip

Chocolate birthday cake

Do you wish you could find a nasty-free cake for the kids' party? If so, this is the recipe for you. Add colour with candles and flags rather than the usual bright sweeties and icing.

TAKES 40 MINUTES, PLUS COOLING • SERVES 12

140g/5oz butter, plus extra for greasing
175g/6oz golden caster sugar
2 large eggs
225g/8oz self-raising wholemeal flour
50g/2oz cocoa powder
½ tsp bicarbonate of soda
250g/9oz natural yogurt
TO DECORATE
300g/10oz golden icing sugar
2 tbsp cocoa powder
1 tbsp butter, melted
3–4 tbsp boiling water
50g/2oz each milk, dark and white chocolate, broken into squares and melted separately

1 Heat the oven to 180C/160C fan/gas 4. Butter and line the base of an 18x 28cm traybake tin. Beat the butter and sugar together until creamy, then add the eggs gradually until fluffy.
2 Sieve the flour, cocoa and bicarbonate of soda into the bowl, then tip in any bran left in the sieve. Stir in the yogurt to a smooth mixture then spoon into the tin. Bake for 20–25 minutes until risen and springy. Cool for 5 minutes, then turn out on to a wire rack.
3 Sieve the icing sugar and cocoa into a bowl, and add the butter and 2 tablespoons of the hot water. Stir together until smooth. Spread over the cold cake using a palette knife dipped in the remaining hot water.
4 Spoon the melted chocolates into separate freezer bags. Snip the ends off then pipe shapes on top of the cake. Once set, cut into squares and push in some candles.

PER SLICE 432 kcals, protein 6g, carbs 65g, fat 18g, sat fat 10g, fibre 3g, sugar 51g, salt 0.41g

Haunted graveyard cake

The base of this cake is like a child-friendly brownie – not too rich, but lovely and moist. You could simply top with some chocolate spread and dark biscuits for gravestones.

TAKES 2¾ HOURS, PLUS COOLING • SERVES 12

85g/3oz cocoa powder
200g/7oz self-raising flour
375g/13oz light muscovado sugar
4 large eggs
200ml/7fl oz milk
175ml/6fl oz vegetable oil
TO DECORATE
1 egg white
50g/2oz icing sugar
200ml/7fl oz single cream
200g/7oz dark chocolate, finely chopped
7 rich tea finger biscuits
100g/3½oz double chocolate cookies, whizzed to crumbs
25g/1oz white chocolate, melted and cooled for 10 minutes
edible silver balls, to decorate

1 Heat the oven to 110C/90C fan/gas ¼. Line a baking sheet with parchment. Whip the egg white until stiff. Gradually whisk in the sugar until stiff and shiny. Spoon into a food bag, cut a 1.5cm hole in one corner then squeeze out 15 ghosts. Bake for 1 hour until crisp.
2 Grease and line a traybake tin (about 20x30x5cm). Turn up the oven to 180C/160C fan/gas 4. For the cake, sift the dry ingredients into a bowl. Beat the wet ingredients together, then stir into the dry until smooth. Pour the cake mix into the tin; bake for 30 minutes then cool.
3 Bring the cream to the boil then stir in the chocolate off the heat. Once smooth, paint thinly over the biscuits. Smooth the rest over the cake. Sprinkle the cake with cookie crumbs.
4 Use white chocolate to stick two silver eyes on to ghosts and pipe on to gravestones. Once set, add the decorations.

PER SLICE 601 kcals, protein 7.5g, carbs 79g, fat 30g, sat fat 9g, fibre 2.5g, sugar 55g, salt 0.52g

Chocolate birthday cake

Haunted graveyard cake

Bread pudding

Turn an old loaf into a nostalgic slice of the past. Bread pudding can be served hot with custard, but it is especially good cold and cut into squares for picnics and lunchboxes.

TAKES 1 HOUR 40 MINUTES, PLUS SOAKING AND COOLING • SERVES 9

500g/1lb 2oz white or wholemeal bread
500g/1lb 2oz mixed dried fruit
85g/3oz cut mixed peel
1 tbsp ground mixed spice
600ml/1 pint milk
2 large eggs, beaten
140g/5oz light muscovado sugar
zest 1 lemon (optional)
100g/3½oz butter, melted
2 tbsp demerara sugar

1 Tear the bread into a large mixing bowl and add the dried fruit, peel and spice. Pour in the milk, then stir or scrunch the mixture through your fingers to mix everything well and completely break up the bread. Add the eggs, muscovado sugar and lemon zest, if using. Stir well, then set aside for 15 minutes to soak.
2 Heat the oven to 180C/160C fan/gas 4. Butter and line the base of a non-stick 20cm-square cake tin (not one with a loose base). Stir the melted butter into the pudding mixture, tip into the tin, then scatter with demerara. Bake for 1½ hours until firm and golden, covering with foil if it starts to brown too much. Turn out of the tin and strip off the paper. Cut into nine large squares and serve warm.

PER SQUARE 510 kcals, protein 10g, carbs 94g, fat 13g, sat fat 7g, fibre 3g, sugar 67g, salt 1.15g

Sticky chocolate-drop cakes

A simple crowd-pleasing cake that will keep well. The fudgy topping is a great recipe to have up your sleeve for children's birthday cakes, too.

TAKES 45 MINUTES, PLUS COOLING • MAKES 15

250g pack unsalted butter, plus extra to grease
300g/10oz golden caster sugar
1 tsp vanilla extract
3 large eggs
200g/7oz self-raising flour
50g/2oz cocoa powder
100g/3½oz mllk chocolate drops
FOR THE TOPPING
85g/3oz butter
85g/3oz golden caster sugar
200g/7oz light condensed milk
50g/2oz milk chocolate drops, plus extra to decorate

1 Butter and line a traybake or small roasting tin, about 20x30cm. Heat the oven to 180C/160C fan/gas 4. Gently melt the butter in a large pan, cool for 5 minutes, then add the sugar, vanilla and eggs, then beat until smooth with a wooden spoon. Stir in the flour, cocoa and ¼ teaspoon salt. Stir in the chocolate drops then bake for 35 minutes until risen all over and an inserted skewer comes out with a few damp crumbs.
2 For the topping, gently heat the butter and sugar together until both are melted. Stir in the condensed milk and bring to the boil. Cool for 5 minutes, then stir in the chocolate drops to melt. Spread over the cold cake, scatter with more chocolate drops and cut into 15 squares.

PER SQUARE 433 kcals, protein 5g, carbs 54g, fat 24g, sat fat 14g, fibre 1g, sugar 42g, salt 0.31g

Sticky chocolate-drop cakes

Bread pudding

Cranberry and poppy seed muffins, page 89

Cupcakes, muffins and other small bakes

Buttermilk scones

Buttermilk adds a lightness that milk alone won't give you.

TAKES 25 MINUTES • MAKES 12

350g/12oz self-raising flour
100g/3½oz caster sugar
85g/3oz butter, cut into small pieces
about 175ml/6fl oz buttermilk or natural
    low-fat yogurt
whipped cream and strawberry jam, to serve

1 Heat the oven to 200C/180C fan/gas 6.
Mix together the flour and sugar in a bowl. Rub the butter in with your fingertips until the mixture resembles fine breadcrumbs. Make a well in the centre of the ingredients and tip in the buttermilk or yogurt, all in one go, then mix lightly to form a soft dough.
2 Tip the dough out on to a lightly floured surface and knead briefly. Press the dough out to a 2.5cm/1in thickness, then stamp out 5cm/2in rounds with a cutter. Gather up the trimmings, knead again briefly and stamp out more rounds.
3 Transfer the scones to a baking sheet, spaced a little apart, and bake for 12–15 minutes until risen and light golden. Leave the scones to cool on a wire rack and serve with the whipped cream and jam.

PER SCONE 187 kcals, protein 3g, carbs 32g, fat 6g, sat fat 4g, fibre 1g, added sugar 9g, salt 0.42g

Blueberry and lemon friands

These light-as-air cakes are sold in every self-respecting coffee shop in Sydney – try them and you too will be hooked.

TAKES 40 MINUTES • MAKES 6

100g/3½oz unsalted butter
125g/4oz icing sugar, plus extra for dusting
25g/1oz plain flour
85g/3oz ground almonds
3 egg whites
grated rind 1 unwaxed lemon
85g/3oz blueberries

1 Heat the oven to 200C/180C fan/gas 6.
Generously butter six non-stick friand or muffin tins. Melt the butter and set aside to cool.
2 Sift the icing sugar and flour into a bowl. Add the almonds and mix everything between your fingers. Whisk the egg whites in another bowl until they form a light, floppy foam. Make a well in the centre of the dry ingredients, tip in the egg whites and lemon rind, then lightly stir in the butter to form a soft batter.
3 Divide the batter among the tins (a large serving spoon is perfect for this job). Sprinkle a handful of blueberries over each cake and bake for 15–20 minutes until just firm to the touch and golden brown. Cool in the tins for 5 minutes, then turn out and cool on a wire rack. To serve, dust lightly with icing sugar.

PER FRIAND 316 kcals, protein 5g, carbs 27g, fat 22g, sat fat 9g, fibre 1g, added sugar 22g, salt 0.09g

Buttermilk scones

Blueberry and lemon friands

Glamorous fairy cakes

The beauty of these little cakes is in their simplicity – a little icing sugar and a sugar flower turn a basic fairy cake into a chic little something.

**TAKES 30 MINUTES, PLUS COOLING •
MAKES 24**

140g/5oz butter, very well softened
140g/5oz golden caster sugar
3 medium eggs
100g/3½oz self-raising flour
25g/1oz custard powder or cornflour
TO DECORATE
600g/1lb 5oz icing sugar, sifted
6 tbsp water
green and pink food colourings
crystallised violets, roses or rose petals
edible wafer flowers

1 Heat the oven to 190C/170C fan/gas 5 and arrange paper cases in two 12-hole bun tins. Put all the cake ingredients in a large bowl and beat for about 2 minutes until smooth. Divide the mixture among the cases so they are half filled and bake for 12–15 minutes, until risen and golden. Cool on a wire rack.
2 Mix the icing sugar and water, and use to top eight cakes. Split the remaining icing and colour it with pink and green colouring. Use to top the remaining cakes then finish each cake with a flower or petal.

PER CAKE 193 kcals, protein 2g, carbs 36g, fat 6g, sat fat 3g, fibre none, added sugar 31g, salt 0.2g

Easy chocolate cupcakes

These light cakes are perfect for freezing before icing – they just need a quick blast in the microwave to bring them back to life.

TAKES 35 MINUTES, PLUS COOLING • MAKES 10

300g/10oz dark chocolate, broken into chunks (you don't need to use one with a high cocoa content)
200g/7oz self-raising flour
200g/7oz light muscovado sugar, plus 3 tbsp extra
6 tbsp cocoa powder
150ml/¼ pint sunflower oil, plus a little extra for greasing
284ml pot soured cream
2 large eggs
1 tsp vanilla extract

1 Heat the oven to 180C/160C fan/gas 4 and line 10 holes of a 12-hole muffin tin with paper cases. Whizz the chocolate into small pieces in a food processor.
2 Take a large mixing bowl and tip in the flour, sugar, cocoa, oil, 100ml/3½fl oz of the soured cream, the eggs, vanilla and 100ml/3½fl oz water. Whisk everything together with electric beaters until smooth, then quickly stir in 100g/3½oz of the whizzed-up chocolate bits. Divide among the cases, then bake for 20 minutes until a skewer inserted into the centre comes out clean (make sure you don't poke it into a chocolate-chip bit). Cool on a wire rack.
3 To make the icing, put the remaining chocolate, soured cream and 3 tablespoons sugar in a small pan. Heat gently, stirring, until the chocolate is melted and you have a smooth icing. Chill in the fridge until firm enough to swirl on top of the cakes, then tuck in.

PER CAKE 534 kcals, protein 6g, carbs 62g, fat 31g, sat fat 11g, fibre 2g, sugar 46g, salt 0.3g

Easy chocolate cupcakes

Glamorous fairy cakes

Gooseberry gems

If you're cooking this recipe out of gooseberry season, frozen berries work just as well.

**TAKES 30 MINUTES, PLUS COOLING •
MAKES 12**

225g/8oz self-raising flour
1 tsp baking powder
200g/7oz golden caster sugar
3 large eggs
150g pot natural yogurt
4 tbsp elderflower cordial
175g/6oz butter, melted and cooled
FOR THE FOOL
350g/12oz gooseberries, topped and tailed,
    or use frozen
50g/2oz golden caster sugar
1 tbsp elderflower cordial
200ml pot crème fraîche
icing sugar, for dusting

1 Heat the oven to 200C/180C fan/gas 6. Line a 12-hole muffin tin with paper cases. Mix the dry ingredients together in a large bowl. Beat the eggs, yogurt, elderflower cordial and melted butter with a pinch of salt, then stir into the dry ingredients. Spoon into the cases, bake for 18–20 minutes until risen and golden, then cool on a wire rack.
2 Gently cook the gooseberries with the sugar in a pan for 10 minutes until the berries have collapsed a little. Stir in the cordial, taste and add more sugar, if you like, then cool. Fold into the crème fraîche.
3 To serve, cut a heart from the top of each cake using a small serrated knife or, if that's too fiddly, simply cut off the top and cut it in half, like a butterfly cake. Spoon a little fool into each cake, top with the piece that you cut away, then dust with a little icing sugar.

PER CAKE 370 kcals, protein 5g, carbs 43g, fat 21g, sat fat 13g, fibre 1g, sugar 29g, salt 0.61g

Blackberry fairy cakes

These little cakes are easy – fun to make and decorate with the kids.

TAKES 35 MINUTES • MAKES 18

150g pot low-fat natural yogurt (rinse the pot
    and use as a measure)
1 pot caster sugar
1 pot sunflower oil
2 eggs
2 pots self-raising flour
250g punnet blackberries, plus extra for
    decorating
finely grated rind 1 orange
FOR THE ICING AND DECORATION
1 pot icing sugar, plus extra for dusting
1 tbsp orange juice
orange food colouring (optional)
50g bar dark chocolate, melted

1 Heat the oven to 190C/170C fan/gas 5. Line two bun tins with 18 paper cases. Tip the yogurt, sugar, oil and eggs into a bowl and whisk until combined. Tip in the flour, three quarters of the blackberries and half the orange rind; fold into the mixture with a large metal spoon – don't overwork.
2 Fill each bun case three-quarters full with the mixture and bake for 20–25 minutes until the cakes are risen and golden. Turn out and cool on a wire rack.
3 Sift the icing sugar into a bowl, add the remaining orange rind and the orange juice to make a smooth icing. Stir in a few drops of orange food colouring, if you like. Using a teaspoon, spoon a little icing on top of each cooled cake. Decorate with extra blackberries, or drizzled melted chocolate.

PER FAIRY CAKE 177 kcals, protein 3g, carbs 29g, fat 7g, sat fat 2g, fibre 1g, added sugar 18g, salt 0.15g

Gooseberry gems

Blackberry fairy cakes

Breakfast munching muffins

Containing marmalade, muesli, orange juice and dried apricots, these muffins make a wonderful start to your day.

TAKES 1 HOUR, PLUS 20 MINUTES SOAKING • MAKES 12

100g/3½oz ready-to-eat dried apricots, chopped
4 tbsp orange juice
2 large eggs
142ml pot soured cream
100ml/3½fl oz sunflower oil
85g/3oz golden caster sugar
300g/10oz self-raising flour, sifted
1 tsp baking powder
50g/2oz crunchy muesli
12 heaped tsp marmalade
FOR THE TOPPING
50g/2oz light muscovado sugar
2 tbsp sunflower oil
50g/2oz crunchy muesli

1 Heat the oven to 190C/170C fan/gas 5. Soak the apricots in the orange juice for 20 minutes or so to plump them up.
2 Beat the eggs in a medium bowl, then mix in the soured cream, oil and sugar. Stir into the apricot mixture. Put the flour, baking powder and muesli in a large bowl, then gently stir in the apricot mixture. Combine thoroughly but quickly – don't overmix or the muffins will be tough.
3 Spoon the mixture into 12 muffin cases (the large paper cases) in a muffin tray. Dip your thumb into a little flour, then make a fairly deep thumbprint in each muffin. Fill each with a heaped teaspoon of marmalade.
4 Combine the topping ingredients and sprinkle over the muffins. Bake for 25–30 minutes, until well risen and golden.

PER MUFFIN 322 kcals, protein 5g, carbs 48g, fat 14g, sat fat 3g, fibre 2g, added sugar 19g, salt 0.51g

Banana and walnut muffins

These deliciously moist muffins use soya flour, and also contain wholemeal flour and sunflower oil to keep them 'heart friendly'.

TAKES 40 MINUTES • MAKES 6

100g/3½oz wholemeal flour
25g/1oz soya flour
3 tbsp caster sugar
2 tsp baking powder
85g/3oz walnuts, roughly chopped
1 egg, beaten
50ml/2fl oz sweetened soya milk
50ml/2fl oz sunflower oil
2 large bananas, about 200g/7oz when peeled, roughly chopped
FOR THE DECORATION
3 tbsp apricot jam
50g/2oz chopped walnuts

1 Heat the oven to 200C/180C fan/gas 6. Line six muffin tins with paper muffin cases or oil the tins. Mix together the first five ingredients in a bowl with a pinch of salt and make a well in the centre.
2 In another bowl, mix together the egg, soya milk and oil. Pour this mixture into the flour and stir until just blended. Gently stir in the bananas. Spoon the mixture into the muffin cases, filling them to about two-thirds full. Bake for 25–30 minutes, until a skewer inserted into the middle comes out clean. Transfer the muffins to a wire rack.
3 Gently heat the jam and brush it on top of the muffins. Sprinkle over the walnuts and serve warm.

PER MUFFIN 425 kcals, protein 9g, carbs 41g, fat 26g, sat fat 3g, fibre 3g, added sugar 17g, salt 0.89g

Banana pecan muffins

If you like the taste of banana loaf, you'll love these moist muffins.

TAKES 40 MINUTES • MAKES 8

250g/9oz plain flour
25g/1oz natural wheatgerm
1 tsp bicarbonate of soda
1 tsp baking powder
½ tsp ground cinnamon
100g/3½oz pecan nuts, roughly chopped
3 small bananas, 350g/12oz total weight in their skins
1 egg, beaten
85g/3oz butter, melted
100g/3½oz light muscovado sugar
175ml/6fl oz buttermilk

1 Heat the oven to 200C/180C fan/gas 6. Butter 8 holes of a muffin tin. In a large bowl, combine the flour, wheatgerm, bicarbonate, baking powder, cinnamon and 85g/3oz pecans. Peel and mash the bananas.
2 In a separate bowl, mix together the egg, butter and sugar, then stir in the mashed banana and buttermilk. Add the egg mixture all at once to the flour mixture, stirring until just combined, but don't overmix or the result will be heavy.
3 Spoon the mixture into the holes to fill. Sprinkle with the remaining pecans. Bake for 20–25 minutes until well risen and golden. Leave in the tin for 10 minutes, then remove and cool on a wire rack.

PER MUFFIN 376 kcals, protein 7g, carbs 47g, fat 19g, sat fat 6g, fibre 2g, added sugar 13g, salt 0.89g

Fruitburst muffins

These low-fat muffins are great to grab when you don't have time to sit down to breakfast.

TAKES 50 MINUTES • MAKES 12

225g/8oz plain flour
2 tsp baking powder
2 large eggs
50g/2oz butter, melted
175ml/6fl oz skimmed milk
100ml/3½fl oz clear honey
140g/5oz fresh blueberries
85g/3oz dried cranberries
140g/5oz seedless raisins
140g/5oz dried apricots, chopped
1 tsp grated orange zest
1 tsp ground cinnamon

1 Heat the oven to 200C/180C fan/gas 6 and very lightly butter a 12-hole muffin tin. Sift the flour and baking powder into a bowl. In another bowl, lightly beat the eggs, then stir in the melted butter, milk and honey.
2 Add the egg mixture to the flour mixture with the remaining ingredients. Combine quickly without overworking (it's fine if there are some lumps left – you want it gloopy rather than fluid). Spoon the mixture into the muffin tin. Bake for 20–25 minutes until well risen and pale golden on top.
3 Leave in the tin for a few minutes before turning out. When cool, they'll keep in an airtight tin for 2 days. They can also be frozen for up to a month.

PER MUFFIN 243 kcals, protein 5g, carbs 41g, fat 8g, sat fat 3g, fibre 2g, added sugar 6g, salt 0.59g

Strawberry and polenta cupcakes

Using polenta and fresh strawberries makes these little cakes especially light and fragrant.

TAKES 35 MINUTES, PLUS COOLING • MAKES 12

140g/5oz unsalted butter, softened
140g/5oz golden caster sugar
zest ½ lemon
85g/3oz polenta
3 large eggs, beaten
140g/5oz plain flour
1 tsp baking powder
1 tbsp milk
140g/5oz strawberries, hulled and chopped
TO DECORATE
3 strawberries, hulled and roughly chopped, plus 6 halved
juice 1 lemon
140g/5oz icing sugar, sifted

1 Line a 12-hole muffin tin with paper cases and Heat the oven to 180C/160C fan/gas 4. Beat together the butter, sugar and lemon zest until pale. Beat in the polenta followed by the eggs, a little at a time.

2 Sift in the flour and baking powder, then fold in quickly with a large metal spoon. Fold in the milk and chopped strawberries. Spoon into the paper cases, then bake for around 20 minutes or until golden and risen. Cool on a wire rack.

3 Peel the cases from the cakes. For the icing, put the chopped strawberries in a bowl with 1 teaspoon of lemon juice and mash to a pulp. Sieve, then add the juice to the sugar to turn it pink. Stir in more lemon juice, drop by drop, to make a thick but flowing icing. Dip each cake into the icing, then top with a strawberry half. Leave to set, then serve.

PER CAKE 271 kcals, protein 4g, carbs 40g, fat 12g, sat fat 7g, fibre 1g, sugar 26g, salt 0.19g

Custard buns

Now here's a new use for that tin of custard powder at the back of the cupboard. The butter should be soft but not greasy for the best result.

TAKES 30 MINUTES, PLUS COOLING • MAKES 12

100g/3½oz custard powder
200g/7oz butter, softened a little
2 large eggs
4 tbsp milk
140g/5oz caster sugar
100g/3½oz self-raising flour, sifted
FOR THE ICING
140g/5oz icing sugar
hundreds and thousands, to decorate

1 Heat the oven to 180C/160C fan/gas 4 and line a 12-hole muffin tin with paper cases. Beat the custard powder with the butter, eggs and milk, then stir in the sugar and fold in the sifted flour. Spoon into the paper cases.

2 Bake for about 20 minutes until a skewer inserted into the centre comes out clean. Leave to cool completely.

3 For the icing, mix the icing sugar with about 3 tablespoons water to form a thick paste. Cover the tops of the buns with the icing, then decorate straight away with hundreds and thousands.

PER BUN 299 kcals, protein 2g, carbs 40g, fat 15g, sat fat 9g, fibre none, sugar 26g, salt 0.45g

Custard buns

Strawberry and polenta cupcakes

Blackberry muffins

Other seasonal berries such as raspberries, loganberries and blueberries also add a delicious fruitiness to these muffins.

TAKES 30 MINUTES • MAKES 12

400g/14oz plain flour
175g/6oz caster sugar
1 tbsp baking powder
finely grated zest 1 orange
½ tsp salt
284ml carton buttermilk
2 eggs, beaten
85g/3oz butter, melted
250g/9oz blackberries

1 Heat the oven to 200C/180C fan/gas 6. Butter a 12-hole muffin tin. In a large bowl, combine the flour, sugar, baking powder, zest and salt. In a separate bowl, mix together the buttermilk, eggs and butter.
2 Make a well in the centre of the dry ingredients and pour in the buttermilk mixture. Stir until the ingredients are just combined and the mixture is quite stiff, but be careful not to overmix. Lightly fold in the blackberries, then spoon the mixture into the tins to fill the holes generously.
3 Bake for 15–18 minutes until risen and pale golden on top. Leave to cool in the tin for a few minutes, as the muffins are quite delicate when hot. Run a palette knife around the edge of the muffins and carefully transfer to a wire rack to cool. Best eaten the same day.

PER MUFFIN 252 kcals, protein 5g, carbs 44g, fat 7g, sat fat 4g, fibre 2g, added sugar 15g, salt 0.79g

Strawberry cheesecake muffins

Each muffin hides a surprise filling of fresh fruit and creamy cheese.

TAKES 40 MINUTES • MAKES 12

350g/12oz plain flour
1½ tbsp baking powder
140g/5oz caster sugar
finely grated rind 2 medium oranges
½ tsp salt
2 eggs
250ml/9fl oz milk
85g/3oz butter, melted
FOR THE FILLING
175g/6oz half-fat soft cheese
3 tbsp caster sugar
6 small strawberries, halved

1 Heat the oven to 200C/180C fan/gas 6. Line a muffin tin with 12 paper cases. Sift the flour and baking powder into a large bowl, then stir in the sugar, orange rind and salt. Beat the eggs and milk together in a jug or bowl, then stir in the butter and gently mix into the dry ingredients to make a loose, slightly lumpy mixture. Do not overmix or the muffins will be tough.
2 Mix together the soft cheese and sugar for the filling. Half-fill the paper cases with the muffin mixture, then push half a strawberry into each. Top with a teaspoon of sweet cheese, then spoon over the remaining muffin mixture to cover and fill the muffin cases.
3 Bake for 15 minutes until well risen and golden on top. Remove from the tin and allow to cool completely on a wire rack.

PER MUFFIN 293 kcals, protein 6g, carbs 42g, fat 12g, sat fat 5g, fibre 1g, added sugar 18g, salt 1.03g

Blackberry muffins

Strawberry cheesecake muffins

Squash, cinnamon and pumpkin seed muffins

This mixture will also divide among a 12-hole muffin tin for smaller muffins.

TAKES 50 MINUTES • MAKES 9

300g/10oz plain flour
1 tbsp baking powder
2 tsp ground cinnamon
1 tsp salt
3 eggs
175ml/6fl oz milk
85g/3oz butter, melted
175g/6oz light muscovado sugar
350g/12oz peeled grated butternut squash
small handful of green pumpkin seeds

1 Heat the oven to 200C/180C fan/gas 6. Lightly butter a 9-hole muffin tin or line with paper muffin cases. Sift together the flour, baking powder, cinnamon and salt and put aside.
2 In a large bowl, mix the eggs, milk and butter. Add the sugar and beat well. Add the flour mixture and beat to give a lumpy batter. Stir in the grated squash.
3 Fill the nine holes of the muffin tin (or paper cases) to the top with the mixture, sprinkle the pumpkin seeds on top. Bake for 20–25 minutes until well risen and firm to the touch. Cool slightly in the tin, turn out and cool on a wire rack.

PER MUFFIN 317 kcals, protein 7g, carbs 50g, fat 12g, sat fat 6g, fibre 2g, added sugar 20g, salt 1.52g

Banana and lemon muffins

Banana chips add extra flavour and a crunchy texture to these muffins.

TAKES 45 MINUTES • MAKES 7

85g/3oz honey-dipped dried banana chips
140g/5oz self-raising flour
2 tsp baking powder
finely grated zest and juice 1 lemon
4 tbsp light muscovado sugar
5 tbsp milk
1 egg, beaten
50ml/2fl oz sunflower oil
3 bananas
4 tbsp icing sugar

1 Heat the oven to 200C/180C fan/gas 6. Lightly oil seven cups of a muffin tin or line with deep paper cases. Break 50g/2oz of the banana chips into pieces. Sift together the flour and baking powder. Stir in the zest, sugar and the broken dried banana chips.
2 Whisk together the milk, egg and oil. Mash the bananas with 1 tablespoon of lemon juice. Fold carefully into the dry ingredients with the egg mixture (do not overwork it). Divide the mixture among the muffin cups/cases, not quite filling them. Bake for 20 minutes until risen and firm. Leave for a few minutes, then transfer to a wire rack to cool.
3 Sift the icing sugar into a bowl. Blend with 1–2 teaspoons of the remaining lemon juice. Drizzle over the muffins; decorate with the remaining whole banana chips.

PER MUFFIN 332 kcals, protein 4g, carbs 57g, fat 11g, sat fat 1g, fibre 1g, added sugar 25g, salt 0.76g

Squash, cinnamon and pumpkin seed muffins

Banana and lemon muffins

Classic blueberry muffins

An easy recipe for light, fluffy blueberry muffins every time.

**TAKES 30 MINUTES, PLUS COOLING •
MAKES 12**

140g/5oz caster sugar
250g/9oz self-raising flour
1 tsp bicarbonate of soda
85g/3oz butter, melted and cooled
2 large eggs, beaten
200ml/7fl oz milk
1 tsp vanilla extract
150g punnet blueberries

1 Heat the oven to 200C/180C fan/gas 6. Line a 12-hole muffin tin with paper cases. In a bowl, combine the dry ingredients. Mix the butter, eggs, milk and vanilla in a jug, pour into the flour mix then stir until just combined. Don't overmix or the muffins will be tough. Fold in the blueberries.
2 Spoon the mixture into the cases and bake for 15–18 minutes until golden and firm. Remove from the tin and cool on a wire rack.

PER MUFFIN 194 kcals, protein 4g, carbs 30g, fat 7g, sat fat 4g, fibre 1g, added sugar 12g, salt 0.68g

Blackberry scones with blackberry jelly and clotted cream

Celebrate late summer's blackberries with this homely scone to tear and share at teatime.

TAKES 35 MINUTES • MAKES 6

50g/2oz butter, cut into small pieces, plus extra
    for greasing
225g/8oz self-raising flour, plus extra for dusting
25g/1oz golden caster sugar
100g/3½oz blackberries
150g pot natural yogurt (not fat free)
4 tbsp milk
blackberry jelly and clotted cream, to serve

1 Heat the oven to 220C/200C fan/gas 7. Line a baking sheet with baking parchment and lightly butter it. Rub the flour and butter together to make rough crumbs. Stir in the sugar, then very gently toss in the blackberries.
2 Mix the yogurt and the milk, pour into a well in the flour mix then very briefly stir together with a round-bladed knife to a soft dough. Flour your hands, then gently gather the dough into a rough ball. Don't knead, or the berries will get too mushy.
3 Put on a lightly floured surface, then gently pat to an 18cm circle about 2cm thick. Transfer to the baking sheet, mark into six wedges, then dust with a little flour. Bake for 18–20 minutes until risen and golden. Break into wedges while warm then serve with the blackberry jelly and clotted cream.

PER SCONE 237 kcals, protein 5g, carbs 37g, fat 9g, sat fat 5g, fibre 2g, sugar 8g, salt 0.55g

Mini coffee cakes

Just the thing with a coffee on a Saturday morning, these cakes are simple to make and sure to please.

**TAKES 45–50 MINUTES, PLUS COOLING •
MAKES 12**

100g/3½oz walnut halves
140g/5oz unsalted butter, softened
140g/5oz caster sugar
3 large eggs, beaten
1 tsp vanilla extract
3 tbsp strong coffee (espresso or made with
    instant), cooled
175g/6oz plain flour
4 tsp baking powder
FOR THE ICING
85g/3oz unsalted butter, softened
140g/5oz icing sugar

1 Heat the oven to 180C/160C fan/gas 4 and line a 12-hole muffin tin with paper cases. Finely chop all but 12 of the walnut halves.
2 Beat the butter and sugar together until pale, then gradually beat in the eggs. Add the chopped walnuts, vanilla and 2 tablespoons of the coffee. Mix the flour and baking powder, fold in gently, then divide the mix among the baking cases. Bake for 15–20 minutes until golden. Cool on a wire rack.
3 To make the icing, beat together the butter and sugar and remaining coffee. Ice the cooled cakes, then decorate with nuts.

PER CAKE 387 kcals, protein 5g, carbs 37g, fat 25g, sat fat 11g, fibre 1g, sugar 25g, salt 0.57g

Cranberry and poppy seed muffins

Serve these muffins warm, drizzled with a generous helping of maple syrup.

TAKES 50 MINUTES • MAKES 10

100g/3½oz unsalted butter
284ml carton soured cream
2 eggs
1 tsp vanilla extract
300g/10oz plain flour
2 tsp baking powder
1 tsp bicarbonate of soda
½ tsp salt
200g/7oz golden caster sugar
4 tsp poppy seeds
140g/5oz fresh or frozen cranberries (thawed)
maple syrup, to serve

1 Heat the oven to 190C/170C fan/gas 5. Line 10 muffin-holes with large discs of very loosely scrunched and lightly oiled greaseproof paper (they should come up the sides of the tin so they become paper muffin cases). Melt the butter, leave to cool for a minute or two, then beat in the soured cream, followed by the eggs and the vanilla extract.
2 In another bowl, mix the flour, baking powder, bicarbonate of soda, salt, sugar and poppy seeds together. Stir this into the soured cream mixture along with the cranberries.
3 Fill each of the prepared muffin cases generously with the mixture and bake for 20–25 minutes. Test with a skewer – it should pull out clean if muffins are done. Lift on to a wire rack, spoon over some maple syrup and eat while they are still warm.

PER MUFFIN 340 kcals, protein 6g, carbs 45g, fat 16g, sat fat 9g, fibre 1g, added sugar 21g, salt 0.98g

Raspberry coffee-time muffins

Make a pot of coffee and enjoy a sweet muffin treat.

TAKES 45 MINUTES, PLUS COOLING • MAKES 12

2 tbsp freshly ground coffee beans
100g/3½oz butter
1 tbsp milk
400g/14oz self-raising flour
50g/2oz pine nuts, half of them toasted
175g/6oz golden caster sugar
1 tsp bicarbonate of soda
2 large eggs
284ml carton buttermilk or soured cream
200–250g/7–9oz fresh raspberries

1 Stir 2 tablespoons boiling water into the coffee. Set aside for a few minutes. Heat the oven to 200C/180C fan/gas 6. Cut out 12 x 10cm squares of baking parchment. Melt the butter, brush a little in each of the holes of a 12-hole muffin tin, then cool the rest slightly. Line the tin with the paper squares, so they stick up a bit. Strain the coffee and mix with the milk.

2 Mix the flour, toasted pine nuts, sugar and bicarbonate of soda in a large bowl. Beat the eggs, buttermilk or soured cream, cooled butter and coffee together. Stir into the flour mix until just combined. Tip in the raspberries, give a few more stirs, then spoon the mix into the tins. They'll be very full.

3 Scatter over the remaining pine nuts, then bake for 25 minutes or until risen and golden. Cool in the tin for a few minutes, then move to a wire cooling rack.

PER MUFFIN 287 kcals, protein 6g, carbs 43g, fat 11g, sat fat 5g, fibre 2g, sugar 18g, salt 0.74g

Triple-chocolate-chunk muffins

Dark, milk and white chocolate melt together to make these muffins completely irresistible.

TAKES 35 MINUTES, PLUS COOLING • MAKES 11

250g/9oz plain flour
25g/1oz cocoa powder
2 tsp baking powder
½ tsp bicarbonate of soda
85g/3oz each dark and white chocolate, broken into chunks
100g/3½oz milk chocolate, broken into chunks
2 large eggs, beaten
284ml pot soured cream
85g/3oz light muscovado sugar
85g/3oz butter, melted

1 Heat the oven to 200C/180C fan/gas 6. Butter 11 holes of a muffin tin. In a large bowl, combine the flour, cocoa and baking powders, bicarbonate of soda and all the chocolate chunks. In a separate bowl, mix together the eggs, soured cream, sugar and butter.

2 Add the soured-cream mixture to the flour mixture and stir until just combined and fairly stiff; don't overmix – the mixture should look quite lumpy. Spoon the mixture into the muffin tin to fill the holes generously.

3 Bake for 20 minutes until well risen. Leave to cool in the tin for about 15 minutes as the mixture is quite soft. Remove from the tin and cool on a wire rack. Eat while still warm and the chocolate is gooey.

PER MUFFIN 325 kcals, protein 6g, carbs 37g, fat 18g, sat fat 11g, fibre 1g, added sugar 17g, salt 0.72g

Triple-chocolate-chunk muffins

Raspberry coffee-time muffins

Simnel egg cupcakes

Get creative over Easter and make some special cupcakes.

TAKES 55 MINUTES, PLUS COOLING • MAKES 12

100g/3½oz butter, softened
100g/3½oz golden caster sugar
2 large eggs
100g/3½oz self-raising flour, plus 1 level tbsp
1 tsp baking powder
1 tsp finely grated orange zest
25g/1oz ground almonds

TO DECORATE

homemade marzipan, to make eggs
edible paste food colours (we used claret, baby blue and primrose yellow)
200g/7oz fondant icing sugar
shimmery hundreds and thousands and sugared almonds, to scatter

1 Heat the oven to 180C/160C fan/gas 4. Line a muffin tin with 12 paper cases. Beat together the butter, sugar, eggs, flour, baking powder and orange zest until smooth and creamy, then fold in the almonds.

2 Spoon the mix into the cases then bake for 20 minutes or until risen and golden and firm to the touch. Cool on a wire rack.

3 To make the marzipan eggs, colour some white marzipan with food colouring then shape into eggs. For the icing, mix the icing sugar with 2 tablespoons water until smooth. Divide among three small bowls and colour one with the claret, one with baby blue and one yellow. Spoon the icing over the cakes and drizzle over the eggs, if you like. Leave to set then scatter with a few hundreds and thousands and a sugared almond or marzipan egg.

PER CAKE 242 kcals, protein 4g, carbs 34g, fat 11g, sat fat 5g, fibre 1g, sugar 27g, salt 0.4g

Fruity spiced swirls

For a change from the norm, roll a simple scone base around autumnal apples and spice. Eat warm, with more butter if you dare.

TAKES 25 MINUTES • MAKES 10

1 tsp ground cinnamon
1 tsp ground nutmeg
3 tbsp demerara sugar
4 tbsp soft butter
1 eating apple, peeled and finely chopped
85g/3oz raisins

FOR THE DOUGH

350g/12oz self-raising flour, plus more for dusting
½ tsp salt
1 tsp baking powder
85g/3oz cold butter, cut into cubes
4 tbsp golden caster sugar
150g pot full-fat natural yogurt
4 tbsp full-fat milk
1 tsp vanilla extract
1 egg beaten with 1 tbsp milk, to glaze

1 Heat the oven to 220C/200C fan/gas 7 and put a baking sheet in to heat. Beat ½ teaspoon of each spice and 2 tablespoons of demerara into the butter, then stir in the fruit.

2 To make the dough, mix the remaining spices, the flour, salt and baking powder in a food processor, then whizz in the butter until it disappears. Pulse in the sugar, tip into a large bowl, then make a well in the middle.

3 Gently warm the yogurt, milk and vanilla together until hot (it may go a bit lumpy looking). Tip it into the well in the bowl and quickly work into the flour with a cutlery knife. As soon as it's all in, stop.

4 Roll the dough to about 40x30cm on a floured surface. Spread with the fruity butter, roll up from the long side, tucking the ends over neatly, then cut into 10 triangles. Brush with the egg glaze and scatter over the remaining sugar. Bake on a floured sheet for 14 minutes.

PER SWIRL 254 kcals, protein 5g, carbs 40g, fat 10g, sat fat 6g, fibre 1g, sugar 17g, salt 0.71g

Simnel egg cupcakes

Fruity spiced swirls

Mother's Day fairy cakes

Decorated with ready-made writing icing and tiny sugar flowers, these little cakes couldn't be easier.

TAKES 30 MINUTES • MAKES 20

FOR THE CAKES
175g/6oz caster sugar
175g/6oz butter, softened
3 eggs, beaten
175g/6oz self-raising flour
1 tsp baking powder
FOR THE DECORATION
140g/5oz icing sugar, sifted
yellow food colouring
selection of writing icings (available in supermarkets)
ready-made sugar flowers (sold with the cake ingredients)

1 Heat the oven to 190C/170C fan/gas 5. Put the cake cases into bun tins. In a bowl, mix all the cake ingredients and beat with an electric whisk for about 1–2 minutes, until evenly mixed.
2 Put a heaped tablespoon of the cake mixture into the centre of each paper case. Bake for 15 minutes, or until golden and well risen. Remove the cakes from the oven and cool on a wire rack.
3 Mix the icing sugar with 4 teaspoons cold water to make a smooth paste, then colour with a drop or two of the yellow food colouring. Spread a teaspoon of the icing on each bun. Leave to set. Using the writing icing, pipe one letter of 'Happy Mother's Day' (or whatever occasion you're celebrating) on to each of the fairy cakes. Leave to set.

PER FAIRY CAKE 186 kcals, protein 2g, carbs 28g, fat 8g, sat fat 5g, fibre trace, added sugar 21g, salt 0.46g

Simnel muffins

Traditional simnel cake can be a bit too rich – instead, try these light little muffins with a gooey nugget of marzipan baked in the centre.

TAKES 55 MINUTES • MAKES 12

250g/9oz mixed dried fruit
grated zest and juice 1 medium orange
175g/6oz butter, softened
175g/6oz golden caster sugar
3 eggs, beaten
300g/10oz self-raising flour
1 tsp ground mixed spice
½ tsp freshly grated nutmeg
5 tbsp milk
175g/6oz marzipan
FOR DECORATING
200g/7oz icing sugar
2 tbsp orange juice for mixing
sugar eggs or mini eggs

1 Tip the fruit into a bowl, add the zest and juice, and microwave on Medium for 2 minutes (or leave to soak for 1 hour). Line 12 deep muffin tins with paper muffin cases. Heat the oven to 180C/160C fan/gas 4. Beat together the butter, sugar, eggs, flour, spices and milk until light and fluffy, about 3–5 minutes. Stir the soaked fruit in well.
2 Half fill the muffin cases with the mixture. Divide the marzipan into 12 equal pieces, roll into balls, then flatten with your thumb. Put one into each muffin case and spoon the rest of the mixture over. Bake for 25–30 minutes, until risen, golden and firm to the touch.
3 Beat together the icing sugar and orange juice to make icing thick enough to coat the back of a wooden spoon. Drizzle over the cooled muffins and top with a cluster of eggs.

PER MUFFIN 465 kcals, protein 6g, carbs 79g, fat 17g, sat fat 8g, fibre 2g, added sugar 42g, salt 0.61g

Mother's Day fairy cakes

Simnel muffins

Date and brown sugar muffins

Everyone will love these muffins for breakfast. They're gluten free but still light and fluffy.

TAKES 35 MINUTES • MAKES 6

50g/2oz butter, plus extra for greasing
50g/2oz dark brown soft sugar, plus extra for sprinkling
2 medium eggs
200ml/7fl oz buttermilk
100g/3½oz quick-cook polenta or fine cornmeal
100g/3½oz rice flour
1 rounded tsp baking powder (most are gluten free but check the pack)
50g/2oz dates, stoned and chopped

1 Heat the oven to 200C/180C fan/gas 6. Butter six holes of a muffin tin. Beat together the butter and sugar until creamy. Beat in the eggs, one at a time, then stir in the buttermilk.
2 Mix the polenta or cornmeal, rice flour and baking powder in a bowl, then fold this into the other mixture. Add the dates.
3 Spoon into the tin and sprinkle with the extra sugar. Bake the muffins for 25–30 minutes until risen and golden.

PER MUFFIN 283 kcals, protein 6g, carbs 44g, fat 10g, sat fat 6g, fibre 1g, added sugar 10g, salt 0.69g

Banana muffins with streusel topping

Full of good-for-you ingredients, these easy muffins would make a great breakfast or lunchbox filler.

TAKES 45 MINUTES, PLUS COOLING • MAKES 6

1 tbsp golden linseed
25g/1oz self-raising flour
15g/½oz butter, at room temperature
40g/1½oz demerara sugar
½ tsp ground cinnamon
FOR THE MUFFINS
100g/3½oz plain wholemeal flour
25g/1oz soya flour
3 tbsp light muscovado sugar
2 tsp baking powder
1 large egg
50ml/2fl oz soya milk
50ml/2fl oz sunflower oil
2 medium-size ripe bananas, roughly mashed

1 Heat the oven to 200C/180C fan/gas 6. Line six holes of a muffin tin with paper cases. For the topping, whizz the seeds in a food processor, or put them in a plastic bag and pound them with a rolling pin until crushed. Rub the flour into the butter until the mixture resembles breadcrumbs. Add the linseed, sugar, and cinnamon. Stir in 2 teaspoons cold water and mix well to moisten.
2 To make the muffins, mix the flours, muscovado sugar and baking powder together in a bowl, and make a well in the centre. Beat the egg, soya milk, oil and mashed banana together, then tip into the well. Stir to combine – don't overmix.
3 Spoon into the muffin cases until they are two-thirds full, then sprinkle a little of the streusel mixture over the top. Bake for about 20–25 minutes or until risen and golden.

PER MUFFIN 295 kcals, protein 6g, carbs 39g, fat 14g, sat fat 3g, fibre 3g, added sugar 15g, salt 0.63g

Feel-good muffins

These muffins have the bonus of lots of health-giving ingredients – so enjoy them without guilt!

TAKES 45 MINUTES • MAKES 6–8

175g/6oz self-raising flour
50g/2oz porridge oats
140g/5oz light muscovado sugar
2 tsp ground cinnamon
½ tsp bicarbonate of soda
1 egg, beaten
150ml/¼ pint buttermilk
1 tsp vanilla extract
6 tbsp sunflower oil
175g/6oz stoned prunes, chopped
85g/3oz pecan nuts

1 Heat the oven to 200C/180C fan/gas 6. Butter 6–8 muffin tins or line them with muffin cases. Put the flour, oats, sugar, cinnamon and bicarbonate of soda in a large bowl, then rub everything through your fingers, as if making pastry, to ensure the ingredients are evenly blended.
2 In a separate bowl, beat the egg, then stir in the buttermilk, vanilla and oil. Lightly stir the egg mixture into the flour. Fold in the prunes and nuts.
3 Divide among the tins, filling the cases to the brim, then bake for 20–25 minutes until risen and golden. Serve warm or cold.

PER MUFFIN (for six) 478 kcals, protein 8g, carbs 66g, fat 22g, sat fat 2g, fibre 2g, added sugar 24g, salt 0.66g

Berry buttermilk muffins

Although best made with fresh blueberries, you can make these muffins using the same amount of frozen berries.

TAKES 40 MINUTES • MAKES 12

400g/14oz plain flour
175g/6oz caster sugar
1 tbsp baking powder
finely grated rind 1 lemon
½ tsp salt
284ml carton buttermilk
2 eggs, beaten
85g/3oz butter, melted
250g/9oz fresh or frozen blueberries, or mixed summer fruits, used straight from frozen

1 Heat the oven to 200C/180C fan/gas 6. Butter a 12-hole muffin tin. In a large bowl, combine the flour, sugar, baking powder, lemon rind and salt. In a separate bowl, mix together the buttermilk, eggs and butter.
2 Make a well in the centre of the dry ingredients and pour in the buttermilk mixture. Stir until the ingredients are just combined and the mixture is quite stiff, but don't overmix. Lightly fold in the berries, then spoon the mixture into the tins to fill generously.
3 Bake for about 25 minutes until risen and pale golden on top. Leave to cool in the tin for about 5 minutes before turning out on to a wire rack, as the muffins are quite delicate when hot.

PER MUFFIN 253 kcals, protein 5g, carbs 44g, fat 7g, sat fat 4g, fibre 1g, added sugar 15g, salt 0.91g

Blueberry lemon cakes with cheesecake topping

Cheesecake meets cake in these adorable little bakes that are ideal for tea or as a dessert.

TAKES 35 MINUTES, PLUS COOLING •
MAKES 12

100g/3½oz butter, softened, plus extra
    for greasing
100g/3½oz golden caster sugar
2 large eggs, lightly beaten
zest and juice 1 lemon
140g/5oz self-raising flour
50g/2oz blueberries
FOR THE TOPPING
250ml/9fl oz soured cream
25g/1oz icing sugar
1 large egg
1 tsp vanilla extract

1 Butter a 12-hole muffin tin. Cross over two 1.5cm strips of baking parchment in each hole – they need to stick up a bit from the tin as you'll use them as handles to remove the cakes when they are cooked.
2 Heat the oven to 180C/160C fan/gas 4. Beat together the butter and sugar until pale. Gradually beat in the eggs, then mix in the lemon zest and juice, and fold in the flour.
3 Divide among the muffin holes, smooth the tops then sprinkle a few blueberries over each cake, reserving the rest for later. Bake for 12 minutes then remove from the oven.
4 Whisk the topping ingredients together until smooth. Gently press down the tops, then spoon the topping over each cake. Scatter with the remaining blueberries and bake for 5–7 minutes more.

PER CAKE 252 kcals, protein 3g, carbs 21g, fat 18g, sat fat 10g, fibre none, sugar 12g, salt 0.32g

Raspberry scones

Spread with clotted cream, these scones make the easiest cream tea ever, and they are perfect for a picnic too.

TAKES 30–35 MINUTES, PLUS COOLING •
MAKES 6

225g/8oz self-raising flour
1 tsp baking powder
1 heaped tbsp caster sugar
50g/2oz butter, diced, plus extra for greasing
about 200ml/7fl oz buttermilk
100g/3½oz raspberries
clotted cream, to serve

1 Heat the oven to 220C/200C fan/gas 7 and butter a baking sheet. Sift the flour and baking powder into a bowl then stir in the sugar. Rub in the butter until the mixture resembles breadcrumbs.
2 Make a well in the centre then gradually add enough buttermilk to mix to a soft, but not sticky, dough. Toss in the raspberries and, using your hands, carefully push them into the dough. The fruit will break up a bit and the dough become streaked.
3 Divide the mixture into six, then plop these mounds on to the baking sheet. Bake for 12–14 minutes until golden brown and cooked through. Remove to a wire rack to cool, then tear apart and spread with clotted cream.

PER SCONE 223 kcals, protein 5g, carbs 36g, fat 8g, sat fat 5g, fibre 2g, added sugar 5g, salt 0.8g

Blueberry lemon cakes with cheesecake topping

Raspberry scones

Raspberry cupcakes with orange drizzle

Who could resist a pretty pile of these fruity cupcakes?

**TAKES 35 MINUTES, PLUS COOLING •
MAKES 12**

200g/7oz self-raising flour
2 tsp baking powder
200g/7oz unsalted butter, softened
4 large eggs
200g/7oz caster sugar
3 tbsp milk
50g/2oz ground almonds
zest 1 medium orange
150g punnet raspberries, lightly crushed,
    plus extra to decorate
FOR THE SUGAR CRUST
juice 1 medium orange
4 tbsp caster sugar

1 Heat the oven to 180C/160C fan/gas 4. Line a 12-hole muffin tin with paper cases. Tip the first eight ingredients into a large bowl and beat with an electric whisk until smooth. Fold the crushed raspberries through the batter.

2 Divide the batter among the cases (they should be about half full) and bake for around 20–25 minutes or until golden and just firm. Make the topping by mixing together the orange juice and sugar.

3 Remove the cupcakes from the oven and allow to cool a little. Put on to a wire rack then drizzle each with the orange and sugar crust mix. Top with the extra raspberries to decorate, then serve.

PER CAKE 328 kcals, protein 5g, carbs 37g, fat 19g, sat fat 10g, fibre 1g, sugar 25g, salt 0.44g

Doughnut cupcakes

A great marriage of two sweet classics, these will disappear in no time.

**TAKES 40 MINUTES, PLUS COOLING •
MAKES 12**

200g/7oz softened butter, plus 3 tbsp melted
200g/7oz golden caster sugar
2 large eggs, plus 1 yolk
300g/10oz self-raising flour
100ml/3½fl oz milk
½ tsp baking powder
12 tsp strawberry jam (about ⅓ of a regular jar)
3–4 sugar cubes, roughly crushed

1 Heat the oven to 180C/160C fan/gas 4. Line a 12-hole muffin tin with paper cases. Tip the softened butter, sugar, eggs, flour, milk and baking powder into a large bowl. Beat together just until you have a smooth, soft batter.

2 Fill the cases two-thirds full with the batter, then make a small dip in the top of each one and then spoon in 1 teaspoon of jam. Cover with another tablespoon of cake batter. Bake for 25 minutes until risen and cooked through. Cool on a wire rack.

3 Brush some melted butter over each cake, then simply sprinkle with the crushed sugar and serve. Will keep for up to 2 days in an airtight container.

PER CAKE 363 kcals, protein 4g, carbs 47g, fat 19g, sat fat 11g, fibre 1g, sugar 28g, salt 0.66g

Doughnut cupcakes

Raspberry cupcakes with orange drizzle

Easy fluffy scones

These scones are the business – light but with a nice crusty outside, and ready in under 30 minutes. Add 85g/3oz sultanas or chopped glacé cherries in with the sugar, if you like.

TAKES ABOUT 25 MINUTES • MAKES 9

350g/12oz self-raising flour, plus more for dusting
½ tsp salt
1 tsp baking powder
85g/3oz cold butter, cut into cubes
4 tbsp golden caster sugar
150g pot full-fat natural yogurt
4 tbsp full-fat milk
1 tsp vanilla extract
1 egg beaten with 1 tbsp milk, to glaze

1 Heat the oven to 220C/200C fan/gas 7 and put a baking sheet inside to heat. Put the flour, salt and baking powder into a food processor, and whizz in the butter until it disappears. Pulse in the sugar; tip it all into a large bowl, then make a well in the middle.
2 In a pan over a low heat, warm the yogurt, milk and vanilla together until hot (it may go a bit lumpy-looking). Pour it into the bowl and quickly work into the flour with a cutlery knife. Stop as soon as it's all in.
3 Tip the mix on to a floured surface and fold it over a few times to create a smooth-ish dough. Press out to about 4cm thick, then stamp out four 7cm diameter rounds. Squash the trimmings together then repeat. Brush the tops with egg glaze, scatter flour over the hot sheet, then add the scones. Bake for around 12 minutes until risen and golden.

PER SCONE 233 kcals, protein 5g, carbs 36g, fat 9g, sat fat 5g, fibre 1g, sugar 9g, salt 0.8g

Peach and almond muffins

Peaches and almonds get along famously, but normally in calorific cakes and pastries. These little muffins are low in fat and can be served warm as a pudding with a scoop of something creamy.

TAKES 35–40 MINUTES, PLUS COOLING • MAKES 6

3 large eggs
100g/3½oz golden caster sugar, plus a little extra for sprinkling
few drops of almond extract
25g/1oz butter, melted
100g/3½oz self-raising flour
25g/1oz ground almonds
2 tbsp peach conserve or apricot jam
2 small peaches, halved, stoned and sliced
1 tbsp flaked almonds
half-fat crème fraîche, to serve

1 Heat the oven to 220C/200C fan/gas 7. In a large bowl, use a hand whisk to mix the eggs, sugar and almond extract together for a minute until foamy. Pour in the melted butter and continue to beat until combined. Gently fold in the flour, ground almonds and a pinch of salt.
2 Divide the muffin mixture among six holes of a non-stick muffin tin. Top each with a blob of conserve or jam and arrange a few slices of peach on top. Scatter over the flaked almonds and a little extra sugar, then bake for 20–25 minutes until puffed up and golden. Serve warm with a spoonful of half-fat crème fraîche, or leave to cool. Best eaten the day they're made or frozen while still slightly warm.

PER MUFFIN 245 kcals, protein 7g, carbs 34g, fat 10g, sat fat 3g, fibre 1g, added sugar 17g, salt 0.34g

Easy fluffy scones

Peach and almond muffins

Cherry coconut muffins

Make these if you've got kids over for a tea party – they'll disappear in minutes (the muffins, not the kids). Just be prepared for sticky fingers.

**TAKES 35–45 MINUTES, PLUS COOLING •
MAKES 9**

100g/3½oz butter, softened
100g/3½oz golden caster sugar
2 large eggs, beaten
175g/6oz self-raising flour
5 tbsp milk
½ tsp vanilla extract
2 tbsp desiccated coconut
100g/3½oz glacé cherries, cut into quarters
TO DECORATE
85g/3oz seedless raspberry jam
50g/2oz glacé cherries, cut into quarters
2 tbsp toasted desiccated coconut

1 Heat the oven to 180C/160C fan/gas 4. Line a muffin tin with nine paper cases. Beat the butter and sugar until pale and creamy, then beat in the eggs gradually until fluffy. Fold in the flour, milk, vanilla and coconut until you have a soft dropping consistency. Stir in the cherries.
2 Spoon the mixture into the paper cases and bake for 20 minutes until risen and golden. Lift the muffins out of the tin and sit them on a wire rack to cool slightly.
3 To decorate, tip the jam into a small pan and gently warm, stirring, until melted and smooth. Generously brush the tops of the warm cakes with the jam, stick the quartered cherries on top and sprinkle with the toasted coconut. Serve on the day of making.

PER MUFFIN 313 kcals, protein 4g, carbs 45g, fat 14g, sat fat 9g, fibre 1g, added sugar 23g, salt 0.27g

Carrot and pineapple muffins

Just like a carrot cake, these muffins will keep beautifully moist.

**TAKES 30–35 MINUTES, PLUS COOLING •
MAKES 12**

140g/5oz self-raising flour
85g/3oz wholemeal flour
½ tsp bicarbonate of soda
2 tsp ground cinnamon
150ml/¼ pint sunflower oil
100g/3½oz golden caster sugar
200g/7oz mashed cooked carrot
3 canned pineapple slices, cut into cubes
2 tbsp pineapple juice, from the can
1 large egg
1 tsp vanilla extract
50g/2oz sunflower seeds

1 Heat the oven to 200C/180C fan/gas 6. Cut out a dozen 10cm squares of baking parchment and put them in a 12-hole muffin tin. Sift together the flours, reserving 2 tablespoons of the bran that collects in the sieve, then stir in the bicarbonate of soda, cinnamon and a pinch of salt.
2 In another bowl, beat the oil, sugar, carrot, pineapple cubes and juice, egg and vanilla. Stir the dry mix into the wet, then spoon into the tin. Sprinkle with the bran and a few sunflower seeds. Bake for 20–25 minutes or until an inserted skewer comes out clean. Leave to cool.

PER MUFFIN 239 kcals, protein 4g, carbs 26g, fat 14g, sat fat 2g, fibre 2g, sugar 12g, salt 0.45g

Pear and toffee muffins

These gooey muffins are delicious warm when the toffee is still melty. If you don't eat them straight away, microwave them for about 20 seconds.

**TAKES 35–40 MINUTES, PLUS COOLING •
MAKES 12**

300g/10oz self-raising flour
1 tsp baking powder
2 tsp ground cinnamon
85g/3oz golden caster sugar
250ml/9fl oz milk
2 large eggs, beaten
100g/3½oz butter, melted
2 ripe pears, peeled, cored and cut into
    small chunks
100g/3½oz soft toffees, chopped into pieces
25g/1oz flaked almonds

1 Heat the oven to 200C/180C fan/gas 6. Line a 12-hole muffin tin with paper cases. Tip the flour, baking powder, cinnamon and a pinch of salt into a large bowl, then stir in the sugar. Mix together the milk, eggs and melted butter in a large jug, and pour into the dry mix all at once, along with the pears and a third of the toffee. Stir briefly until just beginning to combine to a lumpy, streaky batter.
2 Spoon the mixture into the cases, then sprinkle with the remaining toffee and the flaked almonds. Bake for 25–30 minutes until the muffins are risen, golden and feel firm when pressed (the molten toffee will be extremely hot so be careful not to touch it). Remove from the tin to a wire rack to cool.

PER MUFFIN 257 kcals, protein 5g, carbs 36g, fat 11g, sat fat 6g, fibre 1g, sugar 15g, salt 0.62g

Oat and honey muffins

A fluffy light muffin, ideal for lunch alongside big chunks of cheese, or as a snack spread with butter and drizzled with extra honey.

TAKES 40 MINUTES • MAKES 8

250g/9oz plain flour
85g/3oz porridge oats
1 tbsp baking powder
½ tsp ground cinnamon
½ tsp salt
85g/3oz raisins
2 eggs, beaten
200ml/7fl oz milk
75ml/2½fl oz vegetable oil
50g/2oz light muscovado sugar
5 tbsp clear honey

1 Heat the oven to 200C/180C fan/gas 6. Butter 8 holes of a muffin tin. In a large bowl, combine the flour, oats, baking powder, cinnamon, salt and raisins. In a separate bowl, mix together the eggs, milk, oil, sugar and honey. Stir this into the flour mixture until just combined, but don't overmix – the mixture should be quite runny.
2 Spoon the mixture into the holes to fill. Bake for 20–25 minutes. Leave in the tin for a few minutes, then turn out on to a wire rack to cool.

PER MUFFIN 349 kcals, protein 7g, carbs 57g, fat 12g, sat fat 2g, fibre 2g, added sugar 16g, salt 1.18g

Chocolate heart muffins

Tempt the one you love with these wicked little chocolate cakes.

**TAKES 35 MINUTES, PLUS COOLING •
MAKES 10**

250g/9oz plain flour
½ tsp bicarbonate of soda
2 tsp baking powder
100g/3½oz caster sugar
100g/3½oz butter
200g/7oz dark chocolate
250ml/9fl oz buttermilk
2 medium eggs
icing sugar, for dusting
chocolate hearts, to decorate (optional)

1 Heat the oven to 200C/180C fan/gas 6. Butter then flour 10 mini-heart baking tins (or 10 holes of a muffin tin).
2 Mix together the dry ingredients in a large bowl. Melt the butter and chocolate together in a pan over a gentle heat. Off the heat, beat in the buttermilk and eggs. Fold the wet ingredients into the dry, but try not to overmix.
3 Spoon the mix into the tins or muffin holes, then bake for 20–25 minutes, until risen and springy. Cool in the tins for 10 minutes, then ease out with a spatula and dust with icing sugar. Decorate with chocolate hearts, if you like.

PER MUFFIN 285 kcals, protein 5g, carbs 39g, fat 13g, sat fat 8g, fibre 1g, sugar 23g, salt 0.51g

Romantic rose cupcakes

If you've been asked to make cupcakes for a wedding or special occasion, try our moist and tasty vanilla and white-chocolate-topped cakes.

**TAKES 30 MINUTES, PLUS COOLING AND
DECORATING • MAKES 12**

150g pot natural yogurt
3 large eggs, beaten
1 tsp vanilla extract
175g/6oz golden caster sugar
140g/5oz self-raising flour
1 tsp baking powder
100g/3½oz ground almonds
pinch of salt
175g/6oz unsalted butter, melted
TO DECORATE
100g/3½oz white chocolate
140g/5oz unsalted butter
140g/5oz icing sugar
36 small sugar roses and leaves, bought or
    homemade
2.5m thin pink ribbon (optional)

1 Line a 12-hole muffin tin with deep paper cases and heat the oven to 190C/170C fan/gas 5. Mix the yogurt, eggs and vanilla in a jug. Mix the dry ingredients in a large bowl and make a well in the centre.
2 Add the wet mix and the butter to the bowl, then quickly fold in with a large metal spoon – don't overwork it. Fill the cases and bake for 18–20 minutes until golden and springy. Cool for 2 minutes then cool completely on a wire rack. Keep in an airtight container for up to 2 days or freeze as soon as possible.
3 For the frosting, melt the chocolate in the microwave on High for 1½ minutes, stirring halfway. Cool. Beat the icing sugar and butter until creamy. Beat in the chocolate. Spread over the cakes or chill and bring back to room temperature before using. Decorate with roses and tie or glue ribbon on, if you like. Keep them cool but don't chill.

PER CAKE 525 kcals, protein 6g, carbs 57g, fat 32g, sat fat 16g, fibre 1g, sugar 47g, salt 0.36g

Chocolate heart muffins

Romantic rose cupcakes

Spooky spider cakes

Get creepy in the kitchen at Halloween with these clever cakes, just the thing for trick-or-treaters or a Halloween party.

TAKES 1 HOUR, PLUS COOLING • MAKES 12

200g/7oz butter, at room temperature
200g/7oz golden caster sugar
200g/7oz self-raising flour
4 large eggs
½ tsp baking powder
1 tsp vanilla extract
6 tbsp chocolate chips or chopped chocolate
TO DECORATE
2 packs liquorice Catherine wheels
12 tbsp chocolate-nut spread
Liquorice Allsorts (the black ones with the white centre)
1 length red bootlace
1 tube black writing icing

1 Heat the oven to 180C/160C fan/gas 4 and line a 12-hole muffin tin with paper cases, preferably brown ones. For the cake, beat everything but the chocolate together until smooth. Stir in the chocolate. Spoon into the cases then bake for 20–25 minutes until golden and risen. Cool on a wire rack.
2 Unravel the liquorice wheels and cut into lengths to make dangly legs. Stick eight into each cake, making small cuts in the sponge with the tip of a sharp knife so they push in really securely.
3 Spoon the chocolate spread on top and spread lightly to make a round spider's body. Now cut the Allsorts to make eyes and the red bootlace to make mouths, then stick them on to the cakes and dot on the icing to make eyeballs. Will keep for up to 2 days in a cool place.

PER CAKE 481 kcals, protein 6g, carbs 63g, fat 24g, sat fat 10g, fibre 1g, sugar 45g, salt 0.64g

Spider web chocolate fudge muffins

Light and chocolatey, these are the perfect Hallowe'en treat.

TAKES 50 MINUTES • MAKES 10

50g/2oz dark chocolate, broken into pieces
85g/3oz butter
1 tbsp milk
200g/7oz self-raising flour
½ tsp bicarbonate of soda
85g/3oz light muscovado sugar
50g/2oz golden caster sugar
1 egg
142ml pot soured cream
FOR THE TOPPING
100g/3½oz dark chocolate, broken into pieces and melted
100g/3½oz white chocolate, broken into pieces and melted

1 Heat the oven to 190C/170C fan/gas 5 and line a muffin tin with 10 paper cases. Heat the chocolate and butter with the milk until melted. Stir and cool.
2 Mix the flour, bicarbonate of soda and both sugars. Beat the egg in another bowl and stir in the soured cream, then pour this on the flour mixture and add the cooled chocolate. Stir just to combine – don't overmix. Spoon into the cases to about three-quarters full. Bake for 20 minutes until well risen. Cool in the tins for a few minutes, then lift out and continue to cool on a wire rack.
3 Spread one muffin with dark chocolate, then pipe four circles of white chocolate on top. Drag a skewer from the centre to the edge to create a cobweb effect. Alternate dark chocolate on white for the opposite effect.

PER MUFFFIN 349 kcals, protein 5g, carbs 45g, fat 18g, sat fat 9g, fibre 1g, added sugar 28g, salt 0.59g

Spider web chocolate fudge muffins

Spooky spider cakes

Campfire cupcakes

These look really impressive but are simple to make. They'll take you back to toasting marshmallows around an open fire.

**TAKES 30 MINUTES, PLUS COOLING •
MAKES 12**

140g/5oz light muscovado sugar
100g/3½oz self-raising flour
50g/2oz cocoa powder
1 tsp baking powder
3 large eggs
125ml/4fl oz vegetable oil
3 tbsp milk
50g/2oz milk chocolate chips
30g pack mini marshmallows

1 Heat the oven to 180C/160C fan/gas 4 and line a 12-hole muffin tin with paper cases. Tip the sugar, flour, cocoa and baking powders into a large bowl. Whisk together the eggs, oil and milk, then stir together with the dry ingredients until well combined. Add the milk chocolate chips.
2 Divide the mixture among the paper cases, then bake for 20 minutes until risen and cooked through. Leave to cool (you can now store them for up to 2 days in an airtight container).
3 Just before serving (either warm from the oven or cold), arrange marshmallows over the tops of the cakes. Heat the grill to medium and pop the cakes under it for 30 seconds, watching them all the time, or until the marshmallows are lightly browned. Remove and eat straight away.

PER CAKE 233 kcals, protein 3g, carbs 25g, fat 14g, sat fat 3g, fibre 1g, sugar 16g, salt 0.27g

Rudolf's snowball carrot muffins

Adding sweet grated carrot and pineapple to muffins means that you don't need loads of sugar for this cute children's bake.

**TAKES 30 MINUTES, PLUS COOLING •
MAKES 12**

425g can pineapple in juice
200g/7oz self-raising flour
1 tsp bicarbonate of soda
85g/3oz golden caster sugar
50g/2oz desiccated coconut
2 large eggs
85g/3oz butter, melted
150g pot natural bio yogurt
175g/6oz grated carrot
TO DECORATE
50g creamed coconut sachet
100g/3½oz icing sugar
50g/2oz desiccated coconut
orange writing icing
crystallized angelica

1 Heat the oven to 200C/180C fan/gas 6 and line a 12-hole muffin tin with paper cases. Drain the pineapple, reserve the juice, then crush the flesh with a fork.
2 Combine the dry ingredients in a large bowl. Beat the eggs, melted butter and yogurt together, and pour into the bowl with the grated carrot and crushed pineapple. Stir until just combined, then spoon into the cases. Bake for 18 minutes or until risen and golden.
3 Mix the creamed coconut with about 5 tablespoons of pineapple juice and stir in the icing sugar. Put the coconut on a plate. Peel the cooled muffins from their cases and put them on a wire rack. Spread the icing over until completely covered (this can get a bit messy), then roll them in the coconut. Dry for a few minutes. Pipe a carrot on the top of each muffin using the writing icing, and add strips of angelica as stalks.

PER MUFFIN 287 kcals, protein 4g, carbs 38g, fat 14g, sat fat 10g, fibre 2g, sugar 25g, salt 0.63g

Campfire cupcakes

Rudolf's snowball carrot muffins

Crunchy-crusted citrus scones

This is a clever twist on a traditional recipe. Ricotta makes the scones lovely and moist, and the orange zest gives a nice citrus kick to the flavour.

**TAKES 20–25 MINUTES, PLUS COOLING •
MAKES 6**

175g/6oz ricotta
finely grated zest 1 orange
100g/3½oz golden caster sugar
200g/7oz self-raising flour, plus extra for
    sprinkling
50g/2oz butter, cubed, plus extra for greasing
1–2 tbsp milk, plus extra for brushing
1 tbsp demerara sugar
cream or butter and lemon or orange curd,
    to serve

1 Heat the oven to 200C/180C fan/gas 6 and grease a baking sheet. Mix the ricotta, orange zest and half the sugar until combined. Sift the flour into another bowl and add the remaining sugar. Rub the butter into the flour mix so it looks like fine crumbs.
2 Stir the ricotta mix into the flour mix, adding a tablespoon or two of milk to get a soft (but not sticky) dough. Tip on to a floured work surface and knead very lightly a few times only. If you over-knead, the scones will be tough. Roll or press the dough to a neat round about 4cm thick. Place it on the baking sheet and mark it into six wedges.
3 Brush with milk, sprinkle with a little flour and the demerara. Bake for 20–25 minutes until well risen and brown. Transfer to a wire rack to cool slightly. Serve warm, with cream or butter and lemon or orange curd.

PER SCONE 299 kcals, protein 6g, carbs 48g, fat 11g, sat fat 6g, fibre 1g, added sugar 20g, salt 0.39g

Cheddar scones

Split and spread the scrumptious savoury scones with butter then top with whatever you like. Try ham and soft cheese or avocado for starters.

TAKES 25 MINUTES • MAKES 12–15

200g/7oz self-raising flour, plus extra for dusting
50g/2oz butter, at room temperature
25g/1oz porridge oats
85g/3oz grated Cheddar, plus extra for topping
    (optional)
150ml/¼ pint milk, plus extra if needed
TO SERVE
butter, plus a topping of your choice

1 Heat the oven to 220C/200C fan/gas 7. Put the flour in a large bowl, then rub in the butter. Stir in the oats and cheese, then the milk. If it feels like it might be too dry and crumbly, add a touch more milk, then bring together to make a soft dough.
2 Lightly dust the work surface with a little flour. Roll out the dough no thinner than 2cm. Using a 4cm plain cutter, firmly stamp out the rounds – try not to twist the cutter as this makes the scones rise unevenly. Re-roll the trimmings and stamp out more.
3 Transfer to a non-stick baking sheet, dust with a little more flour or grated cheese, then bake for 12–15 minutes until well risen and golden. Cool on a wire rack before serving.

PER SCONE 130 kcals, protein 4g, carbs 15g, fat 6g, sat fat 4g, fibre 1g, sugar 1g, salt 0.36g

Welsh rarebit muffins

Muffins are great to make with kids as the batter doesn't need to be perfectly smooth, and they're quick to create together. These tasty cheese muffins make a great change to lunchbox sarnies.

**TAKES 40 MINUTES, PLUS COOLING •
MAKES 12**

225g/8oz self-raising flour
50g/2oz plain flour
1 tsp baking powder
½ tsp bicarbonate of soda
¼ tsp salt
½ tsp mustard powder
100g/3½oz strong Cheddar, half grated,
   half cubed
6 tbsp vegetable oil
150g pot Greek yogurt
125ml/4fl oz milk
1 large egg
1 tbsp Worcestershire sauce

1 Heat the oven to 200C/180C fan/gas 6. Line a 12-hole muffin tin with paper cases. Mix together the self-raising and plain flours, baking powder, bicarbonate of soda, salt and mustard powder in a bowl.
2 In another bowl, mix the cheese, oil, yogurt, milk, egg and Worcestershire sauce. Combine all the ingredients and divide among the muffin cases. Cook for 20–25 minutes until golden. Remove and cool slightly on a wire rack. Enjoy warm or cold.

PER MUFFIN 189 kcals, protein 6g, carbs 19g, fat 11g, sat fat 4g, fibre 1g, sugar 1g, salt 0.79g

Mediterranean scones

New flavours in an old favourite – great for coffee mornings or an afternoon snack.

**TAKES 30–40 MINUTES, PLUS COOLING •
MAKES 8**

350g/12oz self-raising flour, plus extra for
   dusting
1 tbsp baking powder
½ tsp salt
50g/2oz butter, cut into pieces, plus extra for
   greasing
1 tbsp olive oil
8 Italian sun-dried tomato halves, coarsely
   chopped
100g/4oz feta, cubed
10 black olives, pitted and halved
300ml/½ pint full-fat milk
1 egg, beaten, to glaze

1 Heat the oven to 220C/200C fan/gas 7. Butter a large baking sheet. In a large bowl, mix together the flour, baking powder and salt. Rub in the butter and oil until the mixture resembles fine breadcrumbs, then add the tomatoes, feta and olives. Make a well in the centre, pour in the milk and mix with a knife, using a cutting movement, until it becomes a soft 'stickyish' dough. Don't overhandle the dough.
2 Flour your hands and the work surface well, then shape the dough into a round, about 3–4cm thick. Cut into eight wedges and put them well apart on the baking sheet. Brush with beaten egg and then bake for 15–20 minutes until risen and golden. Transfer to a wire rack and cover with a clean tea towel as they cool to keep them soft. These are best served warm and buttered.

PER SCONE 293 kcals, protein 8g, carbs 36g, fat 14g, sat fat 7g, fibre 2g, added sugar none, salt 2g

Christmas pud cupcakes

Add plenty of wow to your Christmas table with these easy chocolate and cherry puds – ideal for those not keen on classic fruit cake.

TAKES ABOUT 40 MINUTES, PLUS COOLING • MAKES 12

140g/5oz butter, plus extra for greasing
50g/2oz dark chocolate, broken into chunks
100ml/3½fl oz soured cream
3 large eggs, lightly beaten
140g/5oz self-raising flour
140g/5oz golden caster sugar
100g/3½oz ground almonds
6 tbsp cocoa powder
1 tsp baking powder
85g/3oz dried sour cherries, plus a few extra
    to decorate
TO DECORATE
250g/9oz icing sugar, sifted
1 tsp custard powder, sifted
12 small bay leaves

1 Heat the oven to 190C/170C fan/gas 5.
Put a 12-hole silicone muffin tray on a baking
sheet or butter a non-stick 12-hole muffin tin and
stick two criss-crossing strips of baking parchment
in each hole.
2 Melt the butter and chocolate together over a
low heat. Cool, then stir in the soured cream and
eggs. Mix the flour, sugar, almonds, cocoa and
baking powders in a bowl. Pour in the chocolate
mix and cherries, and stir until smooth. Spoon into
the muffin holes, then bake for 20 minutes. Cool in
the tin for 5 minutes, then remove to a wire rack.
3 Mix the icing sugar and custard powder with
2 tablespoons water to make a thick icing. Cut off
any rounded muffin-tops, stand upside-down on
the wire cooling rack, then spoon over the icing.
Leave to set, then top with bay leaves and the
remaining cherries. Best eaten on the day.

PER CAKE 413 kcals, protein 6g, carbs 54g, fat 20g, sat fat 10g,
fibre 2g, sugar 42g, salt 0.51g

Little mince pie cakes

Don't just save these for Christmas – they're a fabulous storecupboard-friendly cake that everyone will love.

TAKES 40 MINUTES, PLUS COOLING • MAKES 12

175g/6oz self-raising flour
100g/3½oz light muscovado sugar
1 tsp ground mixed spice
175g/6oz butter, softened
3 large eggs
2 tbsp milk
about 140g/5oz mincemeat
icing sugar, for dusting

1 Heat the oven to 190C/170C fan/gas 5. Line a
12-hole muffin tin with paper cases. Put the flour,
sugar, spice, butter, eggs and milk into a mixing
bowl, and beat with an electric hand whisk or
wooden spoon for about 2–3 minutes until the mix
is light and fluffy.
2 Put a spoonful of cake mix in each paper case,
then a rounded teaspoon of mincemeat. Cover
the mincemeat with another spoonful of cake mix
and smooth.
3 Bake for 15–18 minutes until golden brown
and firm. Dust with icing sugar and serve warm
or cold.

PER CAKE 272 kcals, protein 4g, carbs 33g, fat 15g, sat fat 9g,
fibre 1g, added sugar 19g, salt 0.4g

Little mince pie cakes

Christmas pud cupcakes

Christmas cupcakes

These cupcakes make a great gift and would go down a storm at a Christmas bazaar.

TAKES ABOUT 1½ HOURS, PLUS COOLING • MAKES 12

200g/7oz dark muscovado sugar
175g/6oz butter, chopped
700g/1lb 9oz luxury dried mixed fruit
50g/2oz glacé cherries
2 tsp freshly grated ginger
zest and juice 1 orange
100ml/3½oz dark rum, brandy or fresh
    orange juice
85g/3oz pecan nuts, roughly chopped
3 large eggs, beaten
85g/3oz ground almonds
200g/7oz plain flour, sifted
½ tsp baking powder
1 tsp each ground mixed spice and cinnamon
TO DECORATE
500g pack ready-rolled marzipan
4 tbsp apricot jam, warmed
500g pack fondant icing sugar
sugared almonds and snowflake sprinkles

1 Tip the first seven ingredients into a pan. Slowly bring to the boil, stirring frequently. Reduce the heat and bubble gently for 10 minutes, stirring often. Cool for 30 minutes.
2 Heat the oven to 150C/130C fan/gas 2 and line a 12-hole muffin tin with paper cases. Stir the nuts, eggs and ground almonds into the fruit then add the flour, baking powder and spices. Once evenly mixed, scoop into the cases and level the tops with a wet spoon. Bake for 35–45 minutes, until an inserted skewer comes out clean.
3 Dust the work surface with a little icing sugar then stamp out 6cm rounds from the marzipan. Brush the cooled cakes with jam, top with marzipan and press down lightly.
4 Make the fondant icing as per the packet instructions then spread over the cakes. Decorate with the sugared almonds and snowflakes.

PER CAKE 751 kcals, protein 9g, carbs 119g, fat 28g, sat fat 9g, fibre 3g, sugar 105g, salt 0.44g

Snow-capped fairy cakes

Soft vanilla cupcakes topped with a snowy, mallow frosting are the ultimate treat.

TAKES 35 MINUTES, PLUS COOLING • MAKES 18

175g/6oz butter
175g/6oz golden caster sugar
3 large eggs
200g/7oz self-raising flour
zest 1 orange
1 tsp vanilla extract
4 tbsp milk
FOR THE FROSTING
1 egg white
4 tbsp fresh orange juice
175g/6oz icing sugar
edible gold and silver balls and thinly sliced fruit
    jellies, to decorate

1 Heat the oven to 190C/170C fan/gas 5. Line 18 holes of two 12-hole muffin tins with paper cases. Melt the butter and cool for 5 minutes, then tip into a large bowl with all the cake ingredients. Beat together until smooth.
2 Spoon the cake mixture into the cake cases, filling them three-quarters full. Bake for 15–18 minutes until lightly browned and firm to the touch. Cool on a wire rack.
3 To make the frosting, put the egg white and orange juice into a heatproof bowl, sift in the icing sugar, then set over a pan of simmering water. Using an electric hand whisk, whisk the icing for 7 minutes until it is glossy and stands in soft peaks. Whisk for a further 2 minutes off the heat.
4 Swirl the frosting on to the cakes, then decorate with fruit jellies and a few silver balls. Leave to set.

PER CAKE 211 kcals, protein 3g, carbs 31g, fat 9g, sat fat 5g, fibre none, sugar 22g, salt 0.31g

Christmas cupcakes

Snow-capped fairy cakes

Walnut oat biscuits, page 138

Biscuits and cookies

Shortbread

Unrefined caster sugar and a salted or slightly salted, creamy butter will give the best flavour.

TAKES 50 MINUTES • MAKES 8

150g/6oz plain flour
100g/3½oz slightly salted butter, cut into
    pieces and softened
50g/2oz golden caster sugar
caster sugar, for sprinkling

1 Heat the oven to 150C/130C fan/gas 2. Put the flour in a mixing bowl, add the butter and rub together to make fine crumbs. Stir in the sugar.
2 Work the mixture together until it forms a ball. Turn out on to a work surface and knead briefly until smooth. Roll and pat out on a very lightly floured surface to an 18cm/7in round. Smooth the surface with your hands. Carefully slide the dough on to an ungreased baking sheet and flute the edges. Mark the circle into eight triangles with a knife, not cutting all the way through. Prick the surface all over with a fork.
3 Bake for 30–35 minutes or until cooked. The shortbread should be very pale. While still warm, cut through the markings and sprinkle with caster sugar. Cool before eating.

PER SHORTBREAD 186 Kcals, protein 2g, carbs 22g, fat 10g, sat fat7g, fibre 1g, added sugar 8g, salt trace

Gooey chocolate cherry cookies

If you like American-style cookies, you'll love these pale, chewy delights, studded with cherry bits plus white and dark choc chips.

TAKES 30 MINUTES, PLUS COOLING • MAKES 20

200g/7oz unsalted butter, at room temperature
85g/3oz light muscovado sugar
85g/3oz golden caster sugar
1 large egg
225g/8oz self-raising flour
50g/2oz dark chocolate, 70% cocoa, roughly
    chopped
50g/2oz white chocolate, roughly chopped
85g/3oz undyed glacé cherries, roughly chopped

1 Heat the oven to 190C/170C fan/gas 5. Beat the butter, sugars and egg until smooth, then mix in the flour, chocolates and cherry pieces and ½ teaspoon of salt. Spoon on to baking sheets lined with baking parchment in large, rough blobs – you'll get 20 out of this mix. Make sure they are well spaced as the cookies grow substantially as they bake. The raw dough can be frozen.
2 Bake for 12–14 minutes until just golden but still quite pale and soft in the middle. If baking from frozen, give them a few minutes more. Cool on the sheets for 5 minutes, then lift on to wire racks with a fish slice and leave to cool completely.

PER COOKIE 186 Kcals, protein 2g, carbs 23g, fat 11g, sat fat 6g, fibre 1g, sugar 14g, salt 0.13g

Shortbread

Gooey chocolate cherry cookies

Toffee apple cookies

Bonfire Night is the perfect excuse to try our special chewy cookies. Once you've tried one batch, you'll be baking them all year round.

TAKES 35–45 MINUTES • MAKES ABOUT 24

175g/6oz unsalted butter, at room temperature
140g/5oz golden caster sugar
2 large egg yolks
50g/2oz ground almonds
85g/3oz chewy toffees, roughly chopped
85g/3oz ready-to-eat dried apple chunks,
    roughly chopped
225g/8oz self-raising flour
2 tbsp milk

1 Heat the oven to 190C/170C fan/gas 5. Using an electric whisk, beat together the butter and sugar until pale and creamy.
2 Stir in the egg yolks, ground almonds, toffees, dried apple and flour. Mix well together then roll out into about 24 or so walnut-size balls.
3 Put well apart on two non-stick or lined baking sheets and flatten the balls slightly with your hand. Brush with milk then bake for 8–12 minutes until golden. Leave to firm up for 5 minutes, then transfer to a wire rack and allow to cool completely.

PER COOKIE 148 kcals, protein 2g, carbs 17g, fat 8g, sat fat 5g, fibre 1g, added sugar 7g, salt 0.12g

Pistachio, orange and oat crumbles

These craggy biscuits have a delicious melt-in-the-mouth texture. Store in an airtight container for up to 3 days, if you can resist them for that long!

TAKES 35 MINUTES, PLUS COOLING • MAKES 16

a little oil, for greasing
125g/4oz unsalted butter
125g/4oz caster sugar
1 medium egg
2 tsp vanilla extract
125g/4oz jumbo porridge oats
75g/3oz plain flour
½ tsp baking powder
100g/3½oz shelled pistachio nuts, roughly
    chopped
125g/4oz orange-flavoured dark chocolate,
    cut into chunks

1 Heat the oven to 180C/160C fan/gas 4. Lightly oil two baking sheets. Beat the butter and sugar together in a large bowl until creamy. Beat in the egg, vanilla extract, oats, flour and baking powder until well combined. Stir in the pistachio nuts and chocolate chunks, and mix well.
2 Divide the mixture into 16 and spoon, spaced well apart, on to the baking sheets. Press down slightly with the back of a fork and bake for 15–20 minutes until golden. Allow to cool slightly before transferring to a wire rack to cool completely.

PER BISCUIT 221 kcals, protein 3g, carbs 24g, fat 13g, sat fat 6g, fibre 1g, sugar 13g, salt 0.07g

Toffee apple cookies

Pistachio, orange and oat crumbles

Blueberry and pecan oaties

Make double the quantity of this fruity cookie dough and freeze it so that delicious home-baked biscuits are always close at hand.

TAKES 35 MINUTES, PLUS CHILLING AND COOLING • MAKES 12

175g/6oz plain flour, plus extra for dusting
½ tsp baking powder
85g/3oz porridge oats
175g/6oz golden caster sugar
1 tsp ground cinnamon
140g/5oz cold butter, chopped
70g pack dried blueberries
50g/2oz pecan nuts, roughly broken
1 large egg, beaten

1 Tip the flour, baking powder, oats, sugar and cinnamon into a bowl, then mix well with your hands. Add the butter and rub into the mixture until it has disappeared. Stir in the blueberries and pecans, add the egg, then mix well with a cutlery knife or wooden spoon until it all comes together in a big ball. Lightly flour a work surface, then roll the dough into a fat sausage about 6cm across. Wrap in cling film, then chill in the fridge until solid.
2 Heat the oven to 180C/160C fan/gas 4. Unwrap the dough and thickly slice into 12 discs and arrange on baking sheets. Bake for 15 minutes (or a few minutes more if you've frozen the sliced dough) until golden. Leave on the sheets to harden, then remove and cool completely on a wire rack before tucking in.

PER BISCUIT 274 kcals, protein 4g, carbs 36g, fat 14g, sat fat 7g, fibre 2g, sugar 20g, salt 0.27g

Marmalade and oat cookies

A little marmalade gives these simple cookies a subtle tang.

TAKES 40 MINUTES • MAKES ABOUT 20

200g/7oz butter
175g/6oz brown soft sugar
2 tbsp thin-cut marmalade
2 tsp ground mixed spice
1 tsp ground cinnamon
1 tsp ground ginger
175g/6oz porridge oats
200g/7oz self-raising flour, plus extra for dusting
2 tsp baking powder
175g/6oz dried fruit, try chopped glacé cherries, apricots and sultanas
100g/3½oz nuts, chopped (we used hazelnuts)

1 Heat the oven to 160C/140C fan/gas 3 and line two baking sheets with parchment. Beat together the butter and sugar until light and fluffy. Mix the marmalade together with 2 tablespoons boiling water. Stir into the creamed mix, then add the spices, oats, flour and baking powder. Mix in the fruit and nuts.
2 Dust your hands and the work surface with flour and roll the dough into a long sausage shape. Cut into about 20 discs. Put on the sheets, spacing them out well as they will spread. Bake for about 25 minutes until golden brown.

PER COOKIE 236 kcals, protein 4g, carbs 30g, fat 12g, sat fat 6g, fibre 2g, sugar 16g, salt 0.42g

Marmalade and oat cookies

Blueberry and pecan oaties

Coconut and cashew cookies

Creamed coconut adds richness and flavour to these American-style cookies.

TAKES 35 MINUTES • MAKES 14–16

140g/5oz unsalted cashews, toasted
85g/3oz creamed coconut, grated
175g/6oz plain flour
½ tsp baking powder
140g/5oz butter, softened
125g/4oz dark muscovado sugar
1 tbsp ground ginger
1 egg

1 Heat the oven to 180C/160C fan/gas 4. Split some cashews in half; leave the rest whole. Mix with the coconut and set aside.
2 Blend the remaining ingredients in a food processor to make a smooth, stiff consistency. Set aside 4 tablespoonfuls of the nut mixture; stir the rest into the flour mixture.
3 Put 14–16 heaped tablespoons of the mixture in mounds, well apart, on buttered baking sheets. Flatten slightly with your fingers. Sprinkle with the reserved nut mixture and bake for 10–12 minutes until golden and set at the edges. Leave for a few minutes, then cool on a rack. The cookies will stay fresh for up to 1 week in an airtight container.

PER COOKIE (for fourteen) 262 Kcals, protein 4g, carbs 22g, fat 18g, sat fat 9g, fibre 2g, added sugar 9g, salt 0.34g

Angela's all-American chocolate chunk cookies

There are no clever techniques involved with Angela Nilsen's irresistible cookies – just measure, mix, stir and bake.

TAKES 50 MINUTES • MAKES 12

300g/10oz dark chocolate (about 55% cocoa solids), broken into small chunks
100g bar milk chocolate, broken into small chunks
100g/3½oz light muscovado sugar
85g/3oz butter, softened
100g/3½oz crunchy peanut butter
1 medium egg
½ tsp vanilla extract
100g/3½oz self-raising flour
100g/3½oz large salted roasted peanuts

1 Heat the oven to 180C/160C fan/gas 4. Melt 100g/3½oz of the dark chocolate chunks. Stir, then tip in the sugar, butter, peanut butter, egg and vanilla, and beat with a wooden spoon until well mixed. Stir in the flour, all the milk chocolate chunks, the nuts and half the remaining dark chocolate chunks. The mixture will feel quite soft.
2 Drop big spoonfuls in 12 piles on to 2 or 3 baking sheets, leaving room for them to spread. Stick 2–3 pieces of the remaining dark chocolate chunks into each cookie.
3 Bake for 10–12 minutes until they are tinged very slightly darker around the edges. They will be soft in the middle, but will crisp up as they cool. Cook for longer and you'll have crisper cookies. Leave to cool for a few minutes, then transfer to a wire rack.

PER COOKIE 381 Kcals, protein 7g, carbs 36g, fat 24g, sat fat 10g, fibre 2g, added sugar 27g, salt 0.42g

Coconut and cashew cookies

Angela's all-American chocolate chunk cookies

Smarties cookies

Make these treats for your next birthday party – for kids or adults.

TAKES 20 MINUTES • MAKES 14

100g/3½oz butter, softened
100g/3½oz light muscovado sugar
1 tbsp golden syrup
150g/6oz self-raising flour
85g/3oz Smarties (about 3 tubes)

1 Heat the oven to 180C/160C fan/gas 4. Beat the butter and sugar in a bowl until light and creamy, then beat in the syrup.
2 Work in half the flour. Stir in the Smarties with the remaining flour and work the dough together with your fingers. Divide into 14 balls. Place them well apart on baking sheets. Do not flatten them.
3 Bake for 12 minutes until pale golden at the edges. Cool on a wire rack. These cookies will keep for up to 4 days in an airtight tin.

PER COOKIE 167 kcals, protein 2g, carbs 23g, fat 8g, sat fat 5g, fibre trace, added sugar 13g, salt 0.3g

Oaty cherry cookies

Store any uncooked mixture in the fridge for up to 1 week, or freeze on the day for up to 6 months, defrosting before baking.

TAKES 30 MINUTES • MAKES 18

250g/9oz butter, softened
50g/2oz caster sugar
100g/3½oz light muscovado sugar
150g/6oz self-raising flour
225g/8oz porridge oats
200g/7oz glacé cherries
50g/2oz raisins

1 Heat the oven to 180C/160C fan/gas 4. Line 2 or 3 baking sheets with non-stick baking paper (or bake in batches). In a bowl, beat the butter and sugars together until light and fluffy. Stir in the flour and oats and mix well. Roughly chop three quarters of the cherries, then stir these and the whole cherries and raisins into the oat mixture.
2 Divide the mixture into 18 equal portions. Roughly shape each portion into a ball. Put on the baking sheets well apart to allow for spreading. Lightly flatten each biscuit with your fingertips, keeping the mixture quite rough looking.
3 Bake for 15–20 minutes until the cookies are pale golden around the edges, but still feel soft in the centre. Cool on the baking sheets for 5 minutes, then transfer to a wire rack.

PER COOKIE 249 Kcals, protein 2g, carbs 33g, fat 13g, sat fat 7g, fibre 1g, added sugar 15g, salt 0.36g

Oaty cherry cookies

Smarties cookies

Lemon and sultana cookies

Swap the sultanas for chopped nuts or other dried fruit to vary the recipe for these American-style cookies.

TAKES 30 MINUTES • MAKES 30

350g/12oz plain flour
½ tsp baking powder
½ tsp bicarbonate of soda
140g/5oz butter, cut into small pieces
175g/6oz caster sugar
85g/3oz sultanas
100g/3½oz lemon curd
2 eggs, beaten
FOR THE ICING
100g/3½oz sifted icing sugar
2 tbsp fresh lemon juice

1 Heat the oven to 200C/180C fan/gas 6. Butter 3 baking sheets (or bake in several batches). Sift the flour, baking powder and bicarbonate of soda into a bowl. Add the butter and rub in with your fingertips until the mixture resembles fine breadcrumbs.

2 Stir in the sugar and sultanas, add the lemon curd and eggs and mix to a soft dough. Shape the dough into 30 small balls, about 2.5cm/1in wide, and put on the baking sheets, allowing plenty of space between them so they can spread. Using your fingers, gently press the top of each biscuit to flatten it slightly.

3 Bake for 12–15 minutes until risen and light golden. Leave to cool for 1 minute on the baking sheets, then transfer to a wire rack to cool completely. Blend the icing sugar and lemon juice, then drizzle over each cookie.

PER COOKIE 134 kcals, protein 2g, carbs 23g, fat 5g, sat fat 3g, fibre trace, added sugar 11g, salt 0.2g

Pine nut cookies

Traditionally made with vegetable shortening, this old-fashioned type of cookie dough can also be made into a case for a fruit tart.

TAKES 1 HOUR • MAKES 18

50g/2oz pine nuts, plus a few extra
175g/6oz butter, softened
140g/5oz golden granulated sugar, plus extra
    for sprinkling
seeds from 1 star anise, crushed (optional)
1 egg
250g/9oz plain flour
1 tsp baking powder

1 Toast the pine nuts in a dry, heavy-based pan for 1–2 minutes. Set aside.

2 Put the butter, sugar and star anise seeds, if using, in a food processor and whizz for 1 minute. Scrape down the bowl, then whizz again briefly. Add the egg and whizz again. Tip in the flour and baking powder, and whizz until the mixture forms a dough. Mix in the pine nuts (reserving enough for step 3), then chill for 30 minutes, wrapped in plastic film.

3 Heat the oven to 180C/160C fan/gas 4. Take about 18 walnut-size pieces of dough and press out into 5cm/2in rounds, level but not too neat. Put on the baking sheets and press two pine nuts on the top of each. Bake for 15 minutes until pale golden. Transfer to a wire rack to cool, sprinkle with sugar and serve.

PER COOKIE 176 kcals, protein 2g, carbs 20g, fat 10g, sat fat 5g, fibre trace, added sugar 9g, salt 0.28g

Lemon and sultana cookies

Pine nut cookies

Almond and lemon curd buttons

Hidden inside these crumbly biscuits lies a heart of lemon curd, giving an unexpected burst of flavour. If you're short of time, leave out the lemon curd and just roll and stamp out lemony shortbreads.

TAKES 30 MINUTES, PLUS CHILLING AND COOLING • MAKES ABOUT 20

250g/9oz butter, softened
140g/5oz golden caster sugar, plus extra for sprinkling
1 large egg
1 tsp vanilla extract
zest 2 lemons
300g/10oz plain flour, plus extra for rolling out
100g/3½oz ground almonds
a little milk, to brush and seal
about 3 tbsp lemon curd
flaked almonds, to scatter

1 Heat the oven to 190C/170C fan/gas 5. Beat the butter, sugar, egg, vanilla, zest and a pinch of salt in a large bowl until smooth, then fold in the flour and ground almonds. Shape into two rounds, flatten them, then wrap in cling film and chill for 30 minutes.
2 Roll out one piece of dough on a floured surface until just thicker than a £1 coin, then stamp out rounds with a 7cm cutter. Brush all over with milk, then spoon roughly 20p-size blobs of lemon curd into the middle of half of the rounds.
3 Carefully lay the remaining rounds on top of the lemon curd, then gently press around the edges with your fingers to seal. Scatter with a little caster sugar and the flaked almonds. Bake for 15 minutes until light golden. Cool. Repeat the process with any remaining pastry.

PER BISCUIT 225 kcals, protein 3g, carbs 22g, fat 15g, sat fat 7g, fibre 1g, sugar 10g, salt 0.21g

Chunky choc orange cookies

Eat these moreish cookies while they're still warm – that way the chocolate is still gorgeously gooey in the middle.

TAKES 30 MINUTES • MAKES 18

250g/9oz butter, softened
50g/2oz caster sugar
100g/3½oz light muscovado sugar
300g/10oz self-raising flour
2 tbsp milk
175g/6oz orange-flavoured dark chocolate, very roughly chopped
50g/2oz pecan nuts, very roughly chopped

1 Heat the oven to 180C/160C fan/gas 4. Line 2 or 3 baking sheets with non-stick baking paper (or bake in batches). In a bowl, beat together the butter and sugars until light and fluffy. Stir in the flour and milk, mix well, then stir in the chocolate and nuts.
2 Divide the mixture into 18 equal portions. Roughly shape each portion into a ball. Put on the baking sheets well apart to allow for spreading. Lightly flatten each biscuit with your fingertips, keeping the mixture quite rough-looking.
3 Bake for 15–20 minutes until the cookies are pale golden around the edges, but still feel soft in the centre. Cool on the baking sheets for 5 minutes, then transfer to a wire rack and allow to cool a little more before eating.

PER COOKIE 261 kcals, protein 2g, carbs 28g, fat 16g, sat fat 9g, fibre 1g, added sugar 14g, salt 0.42g

Almond and lemon curd buttons

Chunky choc orange cookies

Simple jammy biscuits

Kids will love to help you make these simple biscuits that need just five storecupboard ingredients.

**TAKES 20–25 MINUTES, PLUS COOLING •
MAKES ABOUT 12**

200g/7oz self-raising flour
100g/3½oz golden caster sugar
100g/3½oz butter
1 large egg, lightly beaten
4 tbsp strawberry jam

1 Heat the oven to 190C/170C fan/gas 5. Rub the flour, sugar and butter together until the mixture resembles breadcrumbs. Alternatively, you can do this in the food processor. Add enough egg to bring the mixture together to form a stiff dough.
2 Flour your hands and shape the dough into a cylinder, about 5cm across. Cut into 12 finger-width slices and put on a large baking sheet. Space them out, as the mixture will spread when baking.
3 Make a small indentation in the middle of each biscuit with the end of a wooden spoon, then drop 1 teaspoon of jam into the centre. Bake for 10–15 minutes until slightly risen and just golden. Cool on a wire rack.

PER BISCUIT 170 Kcals, protein 2g, carbs 25g, fat 8g, sat fat 5g, fibre 0.5g, sugar 13g, salt 0.3g

Jammy coconut mallows

Kids will love to help sandwiching these biscuits with the melted marshmallow.

**TAKES 50 MINUTES, PLUS CHILLING AND
COOLING • MAKES 18**

250g/9oz butter, softened
140g/5oz golden caster sugar
1 large egg
1 tsp vanilla extract
300g/10oz plain flour
100g/3½oz desiccated coconut
FOR THE MIDDLE AND COATING
about 175g/6oz raspberry jam
18 large marshmallows, cut in half across
    the middle
25g/1oz desiccated coconut

1 Heat the oven to 190C/170C fan/gas 5. Beat the butter, sugar, egg and vanilla together with a pinch of salt until smooth. Fold in the flour and coconut to form a dough.
2 On a floured surface, shape the dough into a round, then roll to the thickness of a £1 coin. Cut into 36 rounds using a 6cm cutter. Lift onto baking sheets, then bake for 14 minutes or until light golden. Cool for 2 minutes, then transfer to a wire rack.
3 To sandwich the biscuits, lay half on a baking sheet, under-side up. Put ½ teaspoon of jam on each one, top with a marshmallow half, then bake for 2 minutes until just melted. Quickly top with the remaining biscuits, pressing down so the marshmallow sticks them together and oozes out a bit. Cool for 10 minutes. Put the coconut and remaining jam on to plates, dip the edges in the jam, then roll them in the coconut.

PER MALLOW 140 kcals, protein 1g, carbs 16g, fat 8g, sat fat 6g, fibre 1g, sugar 10g, salt 0.12g

Jammy coconut mallows

Simple jammy biscuits

Anzac biscuits

These delicious biscuits were made to send to the ANZACs (Australian and New Zealand Army Corps) serving in Gallipoli.

TAKES 35 MINUTES • MAKES 20

85g/3oz porridge oats
85g/3oz desiccated coconut
100g/3½oz plain flour
100g/3½oz caster sugar
100g/3½oz butter, melted
1 tbsp golden syrup
1 tsp bicarbonate of soda

1 Heat the oven to 180C/160C fan/gas 4. Put the oats, coconut, flour and sugar in a bowl. Melt the butter in a small pan or microwave and stir in the golden syrup. Add the bicarbonate of soda to 2 tablespoons boiling water, then stir into the golden syrup and butter mixture.
2 Make a well in the middle of the dry ingredients and pour in the butter and golden syrup mixture. Stir gently to incorporate the dry ingredients.
3 Put 20 dessertspoonfuls of the mixture on to buttered baking sheets, about 2.5cm/1in apart to allow room for spreading. Bake in batches for 8–10 minutes until golden. Transfer to a wire rack to cool.

PER BISCUIT 118 Kcals, protein 1g, carbs 13g, fat 7g, sat fat 5g, fibre 1g, added sugar 6g, salt 0.28g

Chocolate-chunk pecan cookies

You can't beat American-style cookies with big chunks of chocolate and nuts. The perfect grown-up biscuit.

TAKES 25 MINUTES, PLUS COOLING • MAKES 12

200g/7oz dark chocolate, 70% cocoa solids, broken into squares
100g/3½oz butter, chopped
50g/2oz light muscovado sugar
85g/3oz golden caster sugar
1 tsp vanilla extract
1 large egg, beaten
100g/3½oz whole pecan nuts
100g/3½oz plain flour
1 tsp bicarbonate of soda

1 Heat the oven to 180C/160C fan/gas 4. Melt 85g/3oz of the chocolate in the microwave on High for 1 minute or in a bowl set over a pan of simmering water. Beat in the butter, sugars, vanilla and egg until smooth, then stir in three-quarters of both the nuts and remaining chocolate, then the flour and bicarbonate of soda.
2 Heap 12 spoonfuls, spaced apart, on two baking sheets (don't spread the mixture), then poke in the reserved nuts and chocolate. Bake for 12 minutes until firm, then leave to cool on the sheets. Can be stored in an airtight container for up to 3 days.

PER COOKIE 294 Kcals, protein 4g, carbs 27g, fat 20g, sat fat 8g, fibre 2g, sugar 17g, salt 0.44g

Anzac biscuits

Chocolate-chunk pecan cookies

Freezer biscuits

These oat-filled biscuits will keep for ages in the freezer and make a great pick-me-up after a long day.

TAKES 30 MINUTES, PLUS COOLING • MAKES ABOUT 30

250g pack butter, softened
200g/7oz brown soft sugar
1 tsp vanilla extract
2 large eggs
200g/7oz self-raising flour
140g/5oz oats
50g/2oz chopped nuts (try pecan nuts, hazelnuts or almonds)
50g/2oz desiccated coconut
50g/2oz raisins or mixed dried fruit

1 Beat the butter and sugar, then beat in the vanilla and the eggs, one at a time. Stir in a pinch of salt, the flour and oats to make a stiff dough. Add the nuts, coconut and dried fruit, and stir through.
2 Tear off an A4-size sheet of greaseproof paper. Spoon half the mix along the middle of the sheet, then pull over one edge of paper and roll up until you get a tight cylinder. Roll until smooth. Twist up the ends, then freeze for up to 3 months. Repeat with the remaining mix.
3 When ready to cook, heat the oven to 180C/160C fan/gas 4 and unwrap the frozen biscuit mix. Using a sharp knife, cut off rounds roughly ½cm wide. If you have difficulty slicing through, dip the knife into a cup of hot water. Space widely apart on a baking sheet, then bake for 15 minutes until golden brown.

PER BISCUIT 138 Kcals, protein 2g, carbs 16g, fat 8g, sat fat 5g, fibre 1g, sugar 8g, salt 0.21g

Walnut oat biscuits

Serve with ripe Taleggio or another soft cheese, such as dolcelatte or Saint André, and a brimming bowl of fresh, juicy strawberries.

TAKES 25 MINUTES • MAKES 15

100g/3½oz butter, softened
85g/3oz light muscovado sugar
1 egg, beaten
50g/2oz porridge oats
50g/2oz walnuts, finely chopped
85g/3oz plain flour
½ tsp baking powder
cheese and strawberries, to serve

1 Heat the oven to 180C/160C fan/gas 4. Butter two baking sheets. In a bowl, beat the butter and sugar for 5 minutes by hand or 2 minutes in the food processor until light and fluffy. Beat in the egg, then stir in the oats, nuts, flour and baking powder.
2 Drop dessertspoonfuls of the mixture, with a little space between, on the baking sheets. Bake for 15 minutes until pale golden, then cool on a wire rack.
3 Serve as described above with the cheese and strawberries. The biscuits will keep fresh in a sealed container for up to a week.

PER BISCUIT 133 Kcals, protein 2g, carbs 13g, fat 9g, sat fat 4g, fibre 1g, added sugar 6g, salt 0.15g

Freezer biscuits

Walnut oat biscuits

Macadamia and cranberry American cookies

These freeze-ahead cookies are completely irresistible and a great recipe to make as gifts or for a cake sale.

TAKES 1 HOUR 10 MINUTES FOR 4–5 BATCHES, PLUS COOLING • MAKES ABOUT 60

3 x 200g white chocolate bars, chopped
200g/7oz butter
2 large eggs
100g/3½oz light muscovado sugar
175g/6oz golden caster sugar
2 tsp vanilla extract
350g/12oz plain flour
2 tsp baking powder
1 tsp ground cinnamon
100g/3½oz dried cranberries
100g/3½oz macadamia nuts, chopped

1 Heat the oven to 180C/160C fan/gas 4. Melt 175g/6oz of the chocolate, then cool. Beat in the butter, eggs, sugars and vanilla, preferably with an electric hand whisk, until creamy. Stir in the flour, baking powder, cinnamon, cranberries, macadamias and 300g/10oz chopped chocolate.
2 Drop 12 small mounds on to a large baking sheet, spacing them well apart, then poke in some of the remaining chocolate, nuts and berries. Freeze now (see step 3) or bake for 12 minutes until pale golden. Leave to harden for 1–2 minutes, then cool on a wire rack. Repeat with the remaining dough.
3 Freeze raw cookie-dough scoops on baking sheets. When solid, pack them into a freezer container, interleaving the layers with baking parchment. Use within 3 months. Bake from frozen for 15–20 minutes.

PER COOKIE 149 Kcals, protein 2g, carbs 18g, fat 8g, sat fat 4g, fibre none, sugar 13g, salt 0.14g

Cranberry rockies

You can easily adapt this recipe to use raisins, sultanas or even chocolate chunks. Best eaten a day or two after baking.

TAKES 35 MINUTES, PLUS COOLING • MAKES 8 LARGE OR 16 SMALL

oil, for greasing
50g/2oz unsalted butter
100g/3½oz self-raising flour
1 tsp ground mixed spice
50g/2oz light muscovado sugar
85g pack dried cranberries
1 small apple, halved, cored and finely diced
1 large egg, beaten
1 tbsp milk
icing sugar, to dust

1 Heat the oven to 180C/160C fan/gas 4 and lightly oil a non-stick baking sheet. Rub together the butter and flour with your fingertips to fine breadcrumbs (or pulse in a food processor). Stir in the rest of the ingredients, except the icing sugar, until you have a soft dough.
2 Drop eight tablespoons or 16 heaped teaspoons of the dough on to the baking sheet, spacing them out well. Bake for 18–20 minutes until golden. Transfer to a wire rack to cool, then dust with plenty of icing sugar. Pack into an airtight container or gift jars.

PER COOKIE (16) 80 Kcals, protein 1g, carbs 12g, fat 3g, sat fat 2g, fibre 1g, added sugar 3g, salt 0.1g

Macadamia and cranberry American cookies

Cranberry rockies

Festive almond biscuits

Light biscuits with a surprise almond filling and orange-scented sugar.

TAKES 1¼ HOURS • MAKES 20

75g/3oz unsalted butter, chilled and cut into pieces
115g/3½oz self-raising flour
75g/3oz ground almonds
100g/3½oz caster sugar
50g/2oz marzipan, cut into 20 cubes
FOR THE ORANGE SUGAR
pared rind 2 oranges
50g/2oz icing sugar

1 Whizz the butter with the flour and almonds to a breadcrumb consistency. Add half the caster sugar; whizz until the mixture starts to cling together, then work lightly into a ball.
2 Thinly roll out half of the dough. Use 6cm/2½in cutters to cut out crescents and stars; put 20 on a buttered baking sheet. Roll the marzipan cubes into sausage- or ball- shaped pieces and lay on the crecents and stars. Top each with matching dough shape and seal the edges. Chill for 30 minutes.
3 Heat the oven to 160C/140C fan/gas 3. Put the orange rind on a baking sheet and bake for 3 minutes; cool. Mix the remaining caster sugar and the icing sugar; toss with the rind. Bake the biscuits for 18–20 minutes; cool on a wire rack. Sprinkle with the orange sugar.

PER BISCUIT 109 kcals, protein 1g, carbs 14g, fat 6g, sat fat 2g, fibre 1, added sugar 9g, salt 0.06g

Storecupboard-friendly Florentines

Try making these as a variation on cornflake cakes – perfect as a gift for the kids to make.

TAKES 25 MINUTES, PLUS COOLING • MAKES ABOUT 25

85g/3oz cornflakes, bashed with a rolling pin to crush a bit
85g/3oz toasted flaked almonds
50g/2oz dried cranberries
50g/2oz glacé cherries, sliced thinly into rounds
397g can condensed milk
140g/5oz milk chocolate, broken into chunks
140g/5oz white chocolate, broken into chunks

1 Heat the oven to 180C/160C fan/gas 4 and line a couple of baking sheets with baking parchment. Tip the crushed cornflakes, almonds, cranberries and cherries into a large bowl, then stir in the condensed milk until all the ingredients are sticky.
2 Spoon about 25 tablespoons of the mixture on to the sheets, and leave lots of room for spreading. Flatten each slightly with the back of a wet spoon and bake for 8–12 minutes until golden brown. Cool on the sheets for about 5 minutes, then carefully turn them upside down and transfer to another sheet of parchment to cool completely.
3 When cool, melt both the chocolates in a bowl set over a pan of simmering water or in the microwave. Spoon or brush the chocolate over the bases of the biscuits with a pastry brush. Leave to set, then serve or box up as presents.

PER FLORENTINE 158 kcals, protein 3g, carbs 21g, fat 7g, sat fat 3g, fibre none, sugar 18g, salt 0.17g

Storecupboard-friendly Florentines

Festive almond biscuits

Fruity biscotti

Italians love their biscotti – dipped into coffee or vin santo, a sweet dessert wine. Making your own is simple and really satisfying.

TAKES 1¼ HOURS, PLUS COOLING • MAKES ABOUT 72

350g/12oz plain flour, plus extra for dusting
2 tsp baking powder
2 tsp ground mixed spice
250g/9oz golden caster sugar
3 large eggs, beaten
coarsely grated zest 1 orange
85g/3oz raisins
85g/3oz dried cherries
50g/2oz blanched almonds
50g/2oz shelled pistachio nuts

1 Heat the oven to 180C/160C fan/gas 4. Line two baking sheets with baking parchment. Mix the flour, baking powder, spice and sugar in a large bowl. Stir in the eggs and orange zest, then bring together with your hands. Add the fruit and nuts, then work them in well.
2 Split the dough into four. With floured hands, roll into sausages 30cm long. Place on to the baking sheets. Bake for 25–30 minutes until the dough is pale but risen and firm. Cool for a few minutes. Meanwhile, turn down the oven to 140C/120C fan/gas 1.
3 Using a bread knife, cut the sausages diagonally into 1cm slices and then lay the slices flat on the baking sheets. Bake for about 15 minutes, turn over, then bake for another 15 minutes until dry and golden. Tip on to a wire rack to cool completely.

PER BISCUIT 50 kcals, protein 1g, carbs 9g, fat 1g, sat fat none, fibre none, sugar 6g, salt 0.06g

Orange and ginger stained-glass biscuits

You'll make a token effort to leave these on the tree, but they won't stay there for long!

TAKES 35 MINUTES, PLUS CHILLING AND COOLING • MAKES 14

sunflower oil, for greasing
175g/6oz plain flour, plus extra to dust
1 tsp ground ginger
zest 1 orange
100g/3½oz butter, cold, cut into chunks
50g/2oz golden caster sugar
1 tbsp milk
12 fruit-flavoured boiled sweets
about 120cm thin ribbon, to decorate
icing sugar, to dust

1 Heat the oven to 180C/160C fan/gas 4. Grease two large non-stick baking sheets with oil. Whizz the flour, ginger, orange zest and butter with 1 teaspoon salt to fine crumbs in a processor. Pulse in the sugar and milk, then turn out and knead briefly until smooth. Wrap, then chill for 30 minutes.
2 Roll the dough to the thickness of a £1 coin on a floured surface. Cut shapes with 7cm cutters, then use 4cm cutters to cut out the middles. Make a hole in the top of each biscuit, then lift them on to the baking sheets.
3 Crush the sweets with a rolling pin, then put the pieces into the middles of the biscuits – they should be level with the top of the dough. Bake for 15–20 minutes or until golden brown and the middles have melted. Leave to harden, then transfer to a wire rack to cool. Thread some ribbon through the hole in the top of each biscuit, then dust with icing sugar.

PER SERVING 160 kcals, protein 2g, carbs 23g, fat 8g, sat fat 5g, fibre 1g, sugar 10g, salt 0.14g

Fruity biscotti

Orange and ginger stained-glass biscuits

Double-ginger gingerbread men

Even the smallest hands can help to make these friendly little fellows.

TAKES 30 MINUTES, PLUS COOLING • MAKES 12 LARGE GINGERBREAD MEN

140g/5oz unsalted butter
100g/3½oz dark muscovado sugar
3 tbsp golden syrup
350g/12oz plain flour
1 tsp bicarbonate of soda
2 tsp ground ginger
1 tsp ground cinnamon
pinch of cayenne pepper (optional)
2 balls stem ginger from a jar, chopped
TO DECORATE
50g/2oz icing sugar
few undyed glacé cherries, halved then
    thinly sliced
2 balls stem ginger, cut into small squares

1 Heat the oven to 200C/180C fan/gas 6. Line two baking sheets with baking parchment. Melt the butter, sugar and syrup in a pan. Mix the dry ingredients in a bowl then stir in the butter mix and chopped ginger to make a stiff-ish dough.
2 When cool, roll to about 5mm thick. Stamp out gingerbread men, re-rolling the trimmings. Lift on to the baking sheets and bake for around 12 minutes until golden. Cool for 10 minutes, then lift on to wire cooling racks.
3 To decorate, mix icing sugar with a few drops of water until thick and smooth. Spoon the icing into a food bag, snip off just the tiniest bit from one of the corners, then squeeze buttons, eyes and a little smile on to one man at a time. Stick on cherry smiles and ginger buttons. Leave to set. Will keep for up to 1 week in an airtight container.

PER BISCUIT 262 kcals, protein 3g, carbs 43g, fat 10g, sat fat 6g, fibre 1g, sugar 20g, salt 0.27g

Lebkuchen

Lebkuchen are traditional German biscuits, especially popular around Christmas time. They're similar to gingerbread in taste, but with a slightly chewy middle.

TAKES 30 MINUTES, PLUS COOLING • MAKES ABOUT 30

250g/9oz plain flour
85g/3oz ground almonds
2 tsp ground ginger
1 tsp ground cinnamon
1 tsp baking powder
½ tsp bicarbonate of soda
pinch each of ground cloves, freshly grated
    nutmeg and ground black pepper
200ml/7fl oz clear honey
85g/3oz butter
zest 1 lemon
FOR THE ICING
100g/3½oz icing sugar
1 egg white, beaten

1 Tip the dry ingredients into a large bowl. Heat the honey and butter in a pan over a low heat until the butter melts, then pour into the flour mixture along with the lemon zest. Mix well until the dough is combined and fairly solid. Cover and leave to cool.
2 Heat the oven to 180C/160C fan/gas 4. Using your hands, roll the dough into about 30 balls, each 3cm wide, then flatten each one slightly into a disc. Divide the biscuits between two baking sheets lined with baking parchment, spacing well apart. Bake for 15 minutes, then cool on a wire rack.
3 To ice the biscuits, mix together the icing sugar, egg white and 1–2 tablespoons water to form a smooth, runny icing. Dip the top of each biscuit in the icing and spread with the back of a knife. Leave to dry out in a warm place. Store in an airtight container for up to a week.

PER BISCUIT 102 kcals, protein 2g, carbs 16g, fat 4g, sat fat 2g, fibre 0.5g, added sugar 9g, salt 0.16g

Double-ginger gingerbread men

Lebkuchen

Golden flapjacks, page 162

Bars and slices

Fruit and nut squares with chocolate drizzle

Something sweet for those times when you need a quick coffee and a burst of energy.

TAKES 1 HOUR, PLUS COOLING • MAKES 12

140g/5oz butter, plus extra for greasing
200g/7oz porridge oats
25g/1oz desiccated coconut
50g/2oz light muscovado sugar
5 tbsp golden syrup
175g/6oz unsalted mixed nuts, such as
    pistachios and peanuts, chunkily chopped
50g/2oz dried cranberries or cherries
100g bar milk or dark chocolate

1 Heat the oven to 180C/160C fan/gas 4. Butter an 18x28cm cake tin and line the base with baking parchment. Mix together the oats and coconut in a bowl. Melt the butter in a pan over a medium heat with the sugar and syrup. Give it an occasional stir until the sugar has dissolved and the butter has melted.

2 Off the heat, stir in the oat mix, nuts and dried fruit. Leave until cold. Cut two-thirds of the chocolate into chunks and stir into the mix. Tip and spread the mixture into the tin. Bake for 25–30 minutes until pale golden. Mark into squares while still warm.

3 When completely cold, cut all the way through. Melt the rest of the chocolate and drizzle it over the bars. Will keep for a week in an airtight container.

PER SQUARE 345 Kcals, protein 6g, carbs 29g, fat 24g, sat fat 10g, .fibre 3.1g, sugar 17g, salt 0.25g

Sticky plum flapjack bars

A more grown-up flapjack, this one. The tangy plums and slightly bitter walnuts balance the sweet, oaty layers perfectly.

TAKES 1 HOUR 20 MINUTES, PLUS COOLING • MAKES 18

450g/1lb fresh plums, halved, stoned and
    roughly sliced
½ tsp ground mixed spice
300g/10oz light muscovado sugar
350g/12oz butter, plus extra for greasing
300g/10oz oats (not jumbo)
140g/5oz plain flour
50g/2oz chopped walnut pieces
3 tbsp golden syrup

1 Heat the oven to 200C/180C fan/gas 6. Tip the plums into a bowl. Toss with the spice, 50g/2oz of the sugar and a small pinch of salt, then set aside to macerate.

2 Gently melt the butter in a pan. In a large bowl, mix the oats, flour, walnut pieces and remaining sugar, then stir in the butter and golden syrup to a loose flapjack mixture.

3 Grease a 20cm-square baking tin. Press half the oaty mix over the base, then spread the plums over in an even layer. Press the remaining oats over the plums so they are completely covered right to the sides of the tin. Bake for 45–50 minutes until dark golden and starting to crisp a little. Leave to cool completely, then cut into 18 little bars. Will keep in an airtight container for 2 days or can be frozen for up to a month.

PER BAR 335 Kcals, protein 3g, carbs 38g, fat 20g, sat fat 11g, fibre 2g, sugar 22g, salt 0.34g

Fruit and nut squares with chocolate drizzle

Sticky plum flapjack bars

Golden orange and walnut flapjacks

This is one of those great treats that you can just sling together and bake.

TAKES 55 MINUTES • MAKES 12

250g/9oz unsalted butter, chopped into pieces
250g/9oz golden caster sugar
175g/6oz golden syrup
425g/15oz porridge oats
50g/2oz walnut pieces
finely grated zest 1 large orange
3 tbsp fine-cut orange marmalade

1 Heat the oven to 180C/160C fan/gas 4, and generously butter a 28 x 18cm/12 x 7in shallow baking tin. Melt the butter, sugar and syrup over a medium heat, stirring all the time. Take off the heat and stir in the oats, walnuts and orange zest. The mixture should be quite soft.
2 Tip the mixture into the tin and level it off. Bake for around 30 minutes, until the edges are golden brown but the centre is still a little soft. Remove from the oven and mark into 12 pieces while it is still warm, cutting halfway through with a knife. Leave to cool.
3 Heat the marmalade with 1 tablespoon water until it becomes syrupy. Brush this glaze over the flapjack mixture and leave to cool before cutting into 12 pieces. They will keep in an airtight tin for up to a week.

PER FLAPJACK 455 kcals, protein 7g, carbs 60g, fat 22g, sat fat 12g, fibre 4g, added sugar 36g, salt 0.12g

Bramley apple, fig and walnut flapjacks

Combining fruit with fibre is a great energy boost.

TAKES 1¼ HOURS • MAKES 9

450g/1lb Bramley apples, peeled and cored
25g/1oz golden caster sugar
grated zest 1 small lemon
100g/3½oz dried ready-to-eat figs, roughly chopped
140g/5oz butter, cut in pieces
50g/2oz light muscovado sugar
140g/5oz golden syrup
250g/9oz porridge oats
½ tsp ground cinnamon
25g/1oz walnuts, finely chopped

1 Heat the oven to 190C/170C fan/gas 5. Slice the apples into a small saucepan and stir in the caster sugar. Bring to the boil, cover and simmer for 10 minutes or until the apple is soft, stirring occasionally. Stir in the zest and figs, and cook for a further 15 minutes, uncovered, stirring often until the figs are softened and the mixture is quite dry. Whizz to a purée in a food processor.
2 Melt the butter, muscovado sugar and syrup in a saucepan, but don't let it boil. Stir in the oats and cinnamon and mix well.
3 Press half the mixture into an 18cm/7in shallow square sandwich tin. Spread the purée on top and cover with the remaining mixture. Sprinkle over the walnut pieces and bake for 25 minutes or until golden. Remove from the oven, mark into squares and cool.

PER FLAPJACK 516 kcals, protein 6g, carbs 66g, fat 27g, sat fat 14g, fibre 5g, added sugar 24g, salt 0.61g

Chewy gooey flapjacks

These are chewier than most flapjacks because of the bananas mashed in with the oats.

TAKES 45 MINUTES • MAKES 18

140g/5oz butter
100g/3½oz light muscovado sugar
2 heaped tbsp golden syrup
350g/12oz porridge oats (not jumbo oats)
1 tsp ground cinnamon
½ tsp baking powder
2 medium, ripe bananas

1 Heat the oven to 180C/160C fan/gas 4. Butter a 23 x 33cm/9 x 13in Swiss roll tin. Melt together the butter, sugar and syrup in a large saucepan over a low heat, then stir in the oats, cinnamon, baking powder and a pinch of salt until well combined. Peel and mash the bananas and add to the mixture, stirring well to combine. Tip into the prepared tin and smooth the surface with the back of a metal spoon.
2 Bake for 20–25 minutes or until the edges are just beginning to turn golden brown. The mixture will feel fairly firm to the touch.
3 Transfer the tin to a wire rack and cut the mixture into bars while still hot. Leave until completely cold before removing with a palette knife.

PER FLAPJACK 176 Kcals, protein 3g, carbs 25g, fat 8g, sat fat 4g, fibre 1g, added sugar 8g, salt 0.23g

Classic flapjacks

The original schooldays classic is still hard to beat!

TAKES 40–45 MINUTES, PLUS COOLING • MAKES 10

175g/6oz butter
100g/3½oz light muscovado sugar
1 generous tbsp golden syrup
225g/8oz porridge oats

1 Heat the oven to 170C/150C fan/gas 3. Grease and line a 20cm-square baking tin with baking parchment. Put the butter, sugar and syrup into a heavy-based pan over a low heat, and stir until everything has melted together into a dark syrup.
2 Off the heat, tip in the oats and stir to coat. Tip and spread the mixture into the tin. Bake for 20–25 minutes – the mixture should be golden brown with slightly more colour around the edges. Take it out of the oven and, while it's still hot, mark out ten bars on the surface. Then, when just warm, cut along the markings.
3 Once completely cold, loosen the edges with a round-bladed knife. Tip out on to a plate or board, peel off the parchment and break into pieces. The flapjacks will keep in a biscuit tin for up to 3 days.

PER FLAPJACK 259 Kcals, protein 4g, carbs 27g, fat 16g, sat fat 9g, fibre 2g, added sugar 12g, salt 0.3g

Granola bars

Big American-style granola bars are top of the list in coffee-to-go shops. Packed with oats, seeds, fruits and nuts, they are the perfect snack food.

TAKES 35 MINUTES, PLUS COOLING • MAKES 9

175g/6oz unsalted butter
140g/5oz clear honey
250g/9oz demerara sugar
350g/12oz porridge oats
1½ tsp ground cinnamon
85g/3oz pecan nuts or walnuts
85g/3oz raisins
85g/3oz dried papaya or mango, chopped
85g/3oz dried apricots, chopped
85g/3oz pumpkin seeds
50g/2oz ground almonds
50g/2oz sesame seeds

1 Heat the oven to 190C/170C fan/gas 5. Line the base of a 23cm-square cake tin with baking parchment. Melt the butter and honey in a pan, then stir in the sugar.
2 Cook over a low heat for 5 minutes, stirring until the sugar has dissolved. Bring to the boil, then boil for 12 minutes, stirring, until thickened into a smooth caramel sauce.
3 Mix together all the remaining ingredients and stir into the sauce until well combined. Spoon into the tin and press down well with the back of a warm, wet spoon. Bake for 15 minutes until just beginning to brown around the edges. Allow to cool.
4 Run a sharp knife around the sides of the tin to loosen. Turn out, then peel off the lining paper. Cool completely and cut into nine bars.

PER BAR 696 kcals, protein 11g, carbs 85g, fat 37g, sat fat 12g, fibre 6g, added sugar 41g, salt 0.06g

Chocolate and ginger nut slices

A no-bake treat. If you use chocolate with 70% cocoa solids you can even cut the mix into tasty slivers to serve with coffee.

TAKES 25 MINUTES, PLUS CHILLING • MAKES 8

100g/3½oz unsalted butter, plus extra for greasing
185g/6½oz dark chocolate
2 tbsp golden syrup
225g/8oz ginger biscuits, crushed
100g/3½oz hazelnuts, toasted and chopped

1 Lightly butter an 18cm-round sandwich tin. Put the butter, 100g/3½oz of the chocolate and the syrup into a heatproof bowl, and set over a pan of simmering water. Stir occasionally, until melted.
2 Remove from the heat and stir in the crushed biscuits and three-quarters of the nuts. Press the mixture into the tin. Melt the remaining chocolate, then spoon on top and sprinkle over the remaining nuts. Chill for at least 1 hour. Cut into slices to serve.

PER SLICE 433 kcals, protein 4g, carbs 39g, fat 30g, sat fat 13g, fibre 2g, added sugar 20g, salt 0.68g

Granola bars

Chocolate and ginger nut slices

Sticky apricot and almond bars

Absolutely delicious with a cup of tea, these bars are also dairy free.

TAKES 55 MINUTES • MAKES 15

100g/3½oz whole blanched almonds
250g/9oz ready-to-eat dried apricots
85g/3oz porridge oats
85g/3oz plain flour
1 tsp baking powder
250ml/9fl oz jar apple sauce
2 tbsp sunflower oil
1 egg, beaten
2 tbsp apricot jam or conserve

1 Heat the oven to 180C/160C fan/gas 4. Oil and line the base of an 18cm/7in square tin. Roughly chop the almonds into fairly large chunks to give a good texture and finely chop the apricots to give a stickiness to the bars.
2 Put all the dry ingredients in a large bowl. Combine the apple sauce, oil and egg, and add to the dry ingredients. Mix until everything is combined and gooey. Spoon the mixture into the prepared tin, level the surface and bake for 40 minutes or until firm and springy to the touch.
3 Allow to cool in the tin for a couple of minutes, then loosen the sides and turn out on to a wire rack. Warm the apricot jam for 2–3 minutes. Then brush over the surface of the cooled bars, cut into 15 bars and enjoy.

PER BAR 145 Kcals, protein 4g, carbs 19g, fat 6g, sat fat 1g, fibre 2g, added sugar 3g, salt 0.13g

Margaret's caramel nut squares

Margaret Fineran, who created this recipe, was a chef at the American Embassy in London.

TAKES 1¼ HOURS, PLUS 4 HOURS FREEZING • MAKES 9

FOR THE PASTRY
175g/6oz plain flour
50g/2oz icing sugar
85g/3oz cold butter, cut into cubes
¼ tsp vanilla extract
1 small egg, beaten
FOR THE FILLING
85g/3oz granulated sugar
175g/6oz clear honey
50g/2oz butter
284ml pot double cream
100g/3½oz pecan nuts, toasted
100g/3½oz flaked almonds, toasted
100g/3½oz whole hazelnuts, toasted
100g/3½oz pistachio nuts, unsalted, toasted
50g/2oz dried cranberries
whipped cream, to serve

1 Heat the oven to 180C/160C fan/gas 4. Whizz together the flour, icing sugar and butter. Add the vanilla and beaten egg and pulse until the pastry comes together. Chill, wrapped in cling film, for 30 minutes.
2 Roll the pastry out on a lightly floured surface and use to line a 23cm/9in square tin. Pre-bake for 7 minutes. Bring the sugar and honey to the boil without stirring. In a separate pan, heat the butter with the cream until hot. When the sugar mixture is boiling, pour in the hot cream and butter, and simmer, stirring, for 2–3 minutes.
3 Mix in the nuts and cranberries. Spoon into the hot pastry case. Return to the oven for 7 minutes. Remove, cool, then cover and freeze for 3–4 hours. Cut into squares, thaw for 30 minutes, and serve with the cream.

PER SQUARE 743 Kcals, protein 10g, carbs 54g, fat 55g, sat fat 19g, fibre 3g, added sugar 31g, salt 0.35g

Margaret's caramel nut squares

Sticky apricot and almond bars

Raspberry and pine nut bars

This easy-mix bar is the perfect bake – all you do is weigh, mix and scatter everything into the tin.

TAKES 1 HOUR • MAKES 12

200g/7oz plain flour
200g/7oz porridge oats
250g pack butter, cut into small pieces and
    softened
175g/6oz light muscovado sugar
finely grated zest 1 lemon
100g pack pine nuts
250g/9oz raspberries

1 Heat the oven to 190C/170C fan/gas 5. Butter a shallow 23cm/9in square tin. Tip the flour, oats and butter into a mixing bowl and work together with your fingers to make coarse crumbs. Mix in the sugar, lemon zest and three quarters of the pine nuts using your hands, then press the mixture together well so it forms large, sticky clumps.
2 Drop about two thirds of the oat mixture into the tin, spread it out and press down very lightly – don't pack it too firmly. Scatter the raspberries on top, sprinkle the rest of the oat mixture over, then the rest of the pine nuts and press everything down lightly.
3 Bake for 35–40 minutes until pale golden on top. Cut into 12 bars with a sharp knife while still warm, then leave to cool in the tin before removing.

PER BAR 391 Kcals, protein 6g, carbs 40g, fat 24g, sat fat 12g, fibre 3g, added sugar 15g, salt 0.41g

Sunshine bars

The solution for any picnic or open-air event – packed with good things and easy to make.

TAKES 25 MINUTES, PLUS 2 HOURS SETTING TIME • MAKES 18

100g/3½oz dried ready-to-eat tropical medley
    or other mixed dried fruits
100g/3½oz porridge oats
50g/2oz puffed rice cereal
85g/3oz desiccated coconut
50g/2oz blanched hazelnuts or shelled peanuts
    or other nuts
50g/2oz sunflower, sesame or pumpkin seeds
100g/3½oz light muscovado sugar
125ml/4fl oz golden syrup
100g/3½oz butter, cut into pieces

1 Chop the tropical medley into pieces using kitchen scissors. Tip the oats, cereal, coconut and fruit into a large bowl and mix well. Put the hazelnuts and sunflower, sesame or pumpkin seeds in a large frying pan with no oil and, over a moderate heat, stir until they are lightly toasted. Leave to cool a little then tip into the bowl and mix.
2 Put the sugar, syrup and butter in a small pan and heat gently, stirring with a wooden spoon until melted, then simmer for 2 minutes until slightly thicker and syrupy. Quickly stir the syrup mix into the dry ingredients, mixing until well blended with no dry patches.
3 Quickly tip into a 20cm/8in square tin and press down with the back of a spoon to even out the surface. Leave to cool and set – about 2 hours. Cut the mixture into 18 bars.

PER BAR 190 Kcals, protein 2g, carbs 22g, fat 11g, sat fat 6g, fibre 2g, added sugar 11g, salt 0.26g

Raspberry and pine nut bars

Sunshine bars

Apple and apricot treacle tart bars

This bar is deservedly a Good Food *favourite.*

TAKES 1½ HOURS • MAKES 12

FOR THE SHORTBREAD BASE
100g/3½oz butter, softened
50g/2oz light muscovado sugar
175g/6oz plain flour
FOR THE FRUIT FILLING
450g/1lb (about 2 medium) cooking apples,
    cored, peeled and chopped
25g/1oz caster sugar
175g/6oz ready-to-eat dried apricots, halved
FOR THE TREACLE TART TOPPING
grated rind 1 orange, plus 1 tbsp juice
200g/7oz golden syrup
8 tbsp porridge oats

1 Heat the oven to 160C/140C fan/ gas 3. Beat the butter and sugar until fluffy. Stir in the flour until smooth. Tip the mixture into a 23cm/9in square tin and press down on the base. Lightly prick with a fork and bake for 15 minutes. Set aside to cool.
2 Put the apples in a pan with the sugar. Cover loosely and cook over a low heat, stirring occasionally, for about 10 minutes or until the apples are pulpy. Add the apricots and cook gently, uncovered, for a further 15 minutes, stirring. Whizz to a purée.
3 Increase the oven heat to 190C/170C fan/gas 5. Spread the filling over the base. Combine the topping ingredients until well mixed. Spread over the filling. Return to the oven for a further 20–30 minutes, until set and pale golden. Cool in the tin before cutting into 12 bars.

PER BAR 251 kcals, protein 3g, carbs 45g, fat 8g, sat fat 5g, fibre 3g, added sugar 20g, salt 0.29g

Muesli fruit and nut bars

You'll probably have most of the ingredients for these bars in the cupboard already. For the best flavour and texture, choose an unsweetened muesli that's not too fruit filled.

TAKES 35 MINUTES, PLUS COOLING • MAKES 12

100g/3½oz butter, plus extra for greasing
100g/3½oz light muscovado sugar
4 tbsp golden syrup
100g pack pecan nuts
350g/12oz unsweetened muesli
1 medium ripe banana, mashed

1 Heat the oven to 180C/160C fan/gas 4. Butter and line the base of an 18x28cm (or 22cm-square) baking tin with baking parchment. Melt the butter, sugar and syrup in a medium pan on a low heat. Stir until the butter has melted and the sugar has dissolved. Cool slightly.
2 Chop half the nuts. Tip the muesli, banana and chopped nuts into the pan, and stir until well covered. Spoon into the prepared tin and press down with the back of the spoon until firmly packed.
3 Scatter with the whole nuts and press lightly into the mixture. Bake for 20–25 minutes until the muesli turns dark golden and the edges have started to crisp. Leave in the tin until cold, then loosen the edges with a knife. Cut into 12 slices. Keep in an airtight container for up to 5 days.

PER BAR 330 kcals, protein 5g, carbs 34g, fat 20g, sat fat 5g, fibre 3g, added sugar 12g, salt 0.24g

Muesli fruit and nut bars

Apple and apricot treacle tart bars

Golden flapjacks

By using different-size tins and varying the cooking time, this recipe can be adapted to suit all tastes.

TAKES 35 MINUTES • MAKES 12

175g/6oz butter, cut into pieces
140g/5oz golden syrup
50g/2oz light muscovado sugar
250g/9oz oats

1 Heat the oven to 180C/160C fan/gas 4. Line the base of a shallow 23cm/9in square tin with a sheet of baking paper if the tin is not non-stick. (Use a 20cm/8in square tin for a thicker, chewier flapjack.) Put the butter, syrup and sugar in a medium pan. Stir over a low heat until the butter has melted and the sugar has dissolved. Remove from the heat and stir in the oats.

2 Press the mixture into the tin. Bake for 20–25 minutes, until golden brown on top (follow the longer cooking time for a crispier flapjack). Allow to cool in the tin for 5 minutes then mark into 12 bars or squares with the back of a knife while still warm. Cool in the tin completely before cutting and removing – cooling prevents the flapjack from breaking up.

PER FLAPJACK 242 kcals, protein 3g, carbs 29g, fat 14g, sat fat 8g, fibre 1g, added sugar 13g, salt 0.38g

Rocky road squares

These little squares are a tempting combination of chewy marshmallows and crunchy nuts, coated with chocolate.

TAKES 15 MINUTES, PLUS 2 HOURS COOLING • MAKES 50

500g/18oz milk or dark chocolate, broken into pieces
10 marshmallows, cut into small pieces
85g/3oz pecan nuts, almonds or walnuts (or a mixture), roughly chopped

1 Line a shallow 20cm/8in square cake tin with baking paper. In a heatproof bowl set over a pan of simmering water, gently melt the chocolate, then stir in the marshmallows and nuts, mixing well.

2 Pour the mixture into the tin and smooth the top. Leave to set for about 2 hours. Dip a sharp knife in hot water and wipe; cut the cooled mixture into 2.5cm/1in squares.

PER SQUARE 67 kcals, protein 1g, carbs 7g, fat 4g, sat fat 2g, fibre trace, added sugar 5g, salt 0.02g

Moccachino slices

These luscious bites are great for coffee lovers, and this all-in-one-pan method means they're simple to make.

**TAKES 45 MINUTES, PLUS COOLING •
MAKES 12**

100g/3½oz butter, plus extra for greasing
225g/8oz dark brown soft sugar
2 large eggs
3 tbsp espresso coffee (or 3 tbsp boiling
    water with 1 tbsp instant coffee)
2 tsp baking powder
125g/4oz plain flour
FOR THE TOPPING
284ml pot soured cream
300g/10oz white chocolate, broken into chunks
4 tsp caster sugar
cocoa powder, to dust

1 Heat the oven to 180C/160C fan/gas 4 and butter and line the base and sides of a baking tin, about 30x23cm, with baking parchment.
2 Melt the butter in a large pan, stir in the sugar and mix well. Take off the heat and stir in the eggs and coffee. Tip in the baking powder and flour, then mix well. Pour into the baking sheet and bake for 20 minutes. Cool, then turn out on to a board.
3 Meanwhile, melt together the soured cream, white chocolate and sugar in a small bowl set over a pan of simmering water. Stir well, then leave to cool for 15 minutes. Spread all over the top of the cake. Shake over the cocoa powder to dust lightly, then leave to set. Cut into 12 slices and serve with a hot drink.

PER SLICE 372 kcals, protein 5g, carbs 45g, fat 20g, sat fat 12g, fibre 1g, sugar 36g, salt 0.51g

Chocolate crunch bars

If you like rocky road squares, you'll really enjoy these. This recipe is endlessly versatile – use any other sweets instead of Turkish delight, and try digestive or ginger biscuits, if you prefer.

TAKES 20 MINUTES, PLUS CHILLING • MAKES 12

100g/3½oz butter, roughly chopped
300g/10oz dark chocolate, broken into squares
3 tbsp golden syrup
140g/5oz rich tea biscuits, roughly crushed
12 pink marshmallows, quartered (use scissors)
2 x 55g bars Turkish delight, halved and sliced

1 Gently melt the butter, chocolate and syrup in a pan over a low heat, stirring frequently until smooth, then cool for about 10 minutes. Line a 17cm-square baking tin with parchment.
2 Stir the biscuits and sweets into the pan until well mixed, then pour into the tin and spread the mixture roughly to level it. Chill until hard, then cut into bars.

PER BAR 294 kcals, protein 2g, carbs 39g, fat 15g, sat fat 9g, fibre 1g, sugar 31g, salt 0.29g

Choc and nut caramel slice

A dark-chocolate topping and melt-in-the-mouth almond shortbread give this classic bake a very special twist.

TAKES 1 HOUR 20 MINUTES, PLUS CHILLING AND COOLING • MAKES 16

140g/5oz unsalted butter, cold and cut into cubes, plus extra for greasing
175g/6oz plain flour
25g/1oz cornflour
50g/2oz golden caster sugar
85g/3oz blanched almonds, toasted then finely chopped
seeds from 1 vanilla pod
FOR THE CARAMEL
200g/7oz golden caster sugar
142ml pot single cream
50g/2oz butter, cubed
FOR THE TOPPING
200g bar dark chocolate (70% cocoa solids)
85g/3oz butter

1 Heat the oven to 160C/140C fan/gas 3. Lightly butter a shallow 20x23cm baking tin. In a large bowl, sift the flours together, stir in the sugar, almonds and a pinch of salt. Rub in the butter and vanilla seeds to make fine crumbs, then press firmly into the tin. Freeze for 5 minutes, then bake for 35–40 minutes. Cool.
2 For the caramel, put the sugar and 100ml/3½fl oz of water in a heavy-based pan, heat gently until the sugar dissolves, then turn up the heat until it turns a very dark amber. Stir in the cream in four additions until smooth – take care as it will bubble up. Stir in the butter and ½ teaspoon salt. Pour over the shortbread and cool.
3 For the topping, melt the chocolate and butter together then pour over the caramel and smooth with the back of a spoon. Chill for at least 30 minutes before cutting into 16 slices.

PER SLICE 361 kcals, protein 4g, carbs 34g, fat 24g, sat fat 13g, fibre 2g, sugar 22g, salt 0.15g

Blackberry and coconut squares

Use fresh or frozen berries for this unforgettably good treat.

TAKES 1 HOUR, PLUS CHILLING AND COOLING • MAKES 12

250g/9oz self-raising flour
25g/1oz oats
300g/10oz light brown soft sugar
200g/7oz cold butter, cut into pieces
75g/3oz desiccated coconut
2 medium eggs, beaten
350g/12oz frozen or fresh blackberries

1 Heat the oven to 180C/160C fan/gas 4. Tip the flour, oats and sugar into a large bowl. Rub the butter into the flour mixture using your fingertips until only small pea-size pieces remain. Stir through the coconut, then fill a teacup with the mixture and set this aside.
2 Stir the eggs into the remaining mixture in the bowl, then spread over the bottom of a lined baking tin, either 31x17cm or 21cm square. Smooth the surface with the back of a spoon, then scatter over the blackberries
3 Scatter over the reserved teacup of mixture and bake for 1 hour–1¼ hours until golden and cooked through (if you poke a skewer in, it should come out with moist crumbs but no wet mixture). Leave to cool, then remove from the tin and cut into 12 squares.

PER SQUARE 347 kcals, protein 4g, carbs 43g, fat 19g, sat fat 12g, fibre 3g, sugar 26g, salt 0.5g

Blackberry and coconut squares

Choc and nut caramel slice

Choc crunchies

This no-bake treat is great for lunchboxes.

TAKES 50 MINUTES • MAKES 8–10

200g/7oz digestive biscuits
100g/3½oz butter
3 tbsp golden syrup
2 tbsp cocoa powder
50g/2oz raisins
100g/3½oz dark chocolate

1 Butter an 18cm/7in sandwich tin. Seal the biscuits in a strong polythene bag and bash into uneven crumbs with a rolling pin.
2 Melt the butter and syrup in a pan (or microwave on High for about 1½ minutes). Stir in the cocoa and raisins, then thoroughly stir in the biscuit crumbs. Spoon into the tin and press down firmly.
3 Melt the chocolate in a heatproof bowl over a pan of simmering water (or microwave on Medium for 2–3 minutes). Spread over the biscuit base and chill for about half an hour. Keeps for up to 1 week wrapped in foil.

PER CRUNCHY (for eight) 327 kcals, protein 3g, carbs 36g, fat 20g, sat fat 11g, fibre 1g, added sugar 17g, salt 0.77g

Chunky chocolate nut flapjacks

This flapjack, bulging with chunks of chocolate and nuts, is brilliant for lunchboxes.

TAKES 45 MINUTES • MAKES 12

200g/7oz oats
25g/1oz desiccated coconut
140g/5oz butter, cut into pieces
50g/2oz light muscovado sugar
5 tbsp golden syrup
100g/3½oz brazil nuts (or cashew nuts), cut into large chunks
50g/2oz almonds, chopped into large chunks
85g/3oz good-quality dark chocolate, broken into large pieces

1 Heat the oven to 180C/160C fan/gas 4. Lightly butter a 23cm/9in square tin and line the base. Mix together the oats and coconut.
2 Put the butter, sugar and syrup in a pan, cook over a low heat, stirring occasionally, until the butter has melted and the sugar dissolved. Remove from the heat and stir in the oat and coconut mixture. Spoon into the tin and press down evenly. Scatter over the nuts and press lightly into the mixture. Stick the chunks of chocolate between the nuts. Bake for 25–30 minutes, or until a pale golden colour.
3 Mark into 12 bars or squares with the back of a knife while still warm, then allow to cool completely before cutting through and removing from the tin.

PER FLAPJACK 325 kcals, protein 5g, carbs 28g, fat 22g, sat fat 10g, fibre 2g, added sugar 15g, salt 0.3g

Choc crunchies

Chunky chocolate nut flapjacks

Freaky fingers

Halloween just got a little more gruesome! If you don't want to use nuts for the fingernails, you can use pieces of glacé cherry instead.

TAKES 25 MINUTES, PLUS CHILLING AND COOLING • MAKES ABOUT 20

100g/3½oz caster sugar
100g/3½oz butter
1 large egg yolk
200g/7oz plain flour
½ tsp vanilla extract
20 blanched almonds
red food colouring, paste is best (optional)

1 Line a baking sheet with parchment. Put the first five ingredients and a pinch of salt in a food processor, and whizz just until a ball of dough forms.
2 Tear off a golfball-size piece of dough and use your hands to roll into a finger-size cylinder. Repeat until you get about 20. Put the biscuits on to the sheet, well spaced apart.
3 Use a knife to make a few cuts, close together, for the knuckles. Put an almond at the end of each finger and trim away excess pastry around the edge. Chill for 30 minutes.
4 Meanwhile, heat the oven to 190C/170C fan/gas 5. When chilled, bake for 10–12 minutes just until firm. Leave to cool a little, then paint the almonds with food colouring, if you like. Can be made up to 3 days ahead and stored in an airtight container.

PER FINGER 102 kcals, protein 1g, carbs 13g, fat 5g, sat fat 3g, fibre none, sugar 6g, salt 0.08g

Squeamish squares

These will be a big hit with children – they're sticky, crunchy and chewy in one bite.

TAKES 20 MINUTES, PLUS CHILLING • MAKES 16 SQUARES OR 32 BITE-SIZE CHUNKS

140g/5oz dark chocolate, broken into pieces (70% cocoa solids is good)
100g/3½oz unsalted butter
4 tbsp golden syrup
100g/3½oz puffed rice cereal
50g/2oz dried blueberries
50g/2oz dried cranberries
100g/3½oz mini marshmallows
50g/2oz white chocolate, broken into pieces
jelly snakes and bugs, to decorate

1 Line a 20cm-square tin with baking parchment. Melt the dark chocolate, butter and golden syrup together in a pan over a low heat.
2 Put the cereal in a large bowl and mix in the blueberries, cranberries and marshmallows. Stir in the melted dark chocolate to coat. Spoon the mixture into the tin and spread out evenly. Chill in the fridge for at least 1 hour until set.
3 Remove from the tin and peel away the paper. Using a sharp knife, cut into 16 squares or 32 bite-size pieces. Melt the white chocolate in a small bowl set over a pan of barely simmering water (or in the microwave on High for 1 minute, stirring halfway through). Using a teaspoon, drizzle the white chocolate over the squares. Scatter with the jelly sweets, then leave to set before serving. Keep in an airtight container for up to 2 days.

PER SQUARE 197 kcals, protein 2g, carbs 26g, fat 10g, sat fat 6g, fibre 1g, sugar 17g, salt 0.15g

Squeamish squares

Freaky fingers

Festive mince pies, page 189

Tarts, pastries and pies

Cinnamon and lemon tarts with berries

These light and luscious tarts are a cross between the traditional Yorkshire curd tart and the lemony Portuguese version.

TAKES 45 MINUTES • SERVES 6

375g pack ready-rolled puff pastry
200g tub light soft cheese
grated rind ½ lemon
100g/3½oz caster sugar
2 egg yolks
1 tbsp plain flour
TO DECORATE
100g/3½oz each of raspberries and blueberries
cinnamon and icing sugar, for dusting
142ml carton single cream (optional)

1 Heat the oven to 200C/180C fan/gas 6. Unwrap the pastry, then roll it out so you can stamp out 12 rounds using an 7.5cm/3in fluted cutter. Line 12 bun tins with the pastry and prick them with a fork all over (this is essential to stop the pastry rising up in the centre and tipping the filling out).
2 Beat the cheese until soft, then beat in the lemon rind, sugar and egg yolks. Sift in the flour and mix well. Pour into the pastry cases, almost to the top.
3 Bake the tarts for 12–15 minutes, until the pastry is golden and the filling lightly coloured. Carefully remove from the tins and leave aside on a rack to cool. To serve, place 2 tarts on a plate, scatter the berries over, dust lightly with cinnamon and icing sugar, then drizzle with a little cream, if you like.

PER SERVING 411 kcals, protein 8g, carbs 48g, fat 22g, sat fat 1g, fibre 1g, added sugar 19g, salt 0.76g

Raspberry and white chocolate slice

This delicious bake has the most wonderful texture. It will keep in the fridge for up to 3 days – leave it on the tin base and cut off slices as you go.

TAKES 40 MINUTES, PLUS COOLING • MAKES 16

375g pack ready-rolled shortcrust pastry
2 x 250g tubs mascarpone
100g/3½oz golden caster sugar
100g/3½oz ground almonds
2 large eggs
250g/9oz fresh raspberries
100g/3½oz white chocolate, roughly chopped

1 Heat the oven to 160C/140C fan/gas 3. Roll out the pastry a little more on a floured work surface and use to line either a 30 x 20cm tin or a Swiss roll tin. Line with greaseproof paper, fill with baking beans and cook for 10 minutes. Take out the beans and paper, then return to the oven for a further 5 minutes.
2 Whisk together the mascarpone, sugar, almonds and eggs until well blended. Fold in the raspberries and chocolate, then pour into the tin. Bake for 20–25 minutes until just set and lightly golden. Turn off the oven, open the door and leave the slice to cool gradually. For the best results, chill for at least 1 hour before slicing into 16 pieces.

PER SLICE 314 kcals, protein 5g, carbs 19g, fat 25g, sat fat 12g, fibre 2g, sugar 13g, salt 0.18g

Cinnamon and lemon tarts with berries

Raspberry and white chocolate slice

Individual strawberry and almond tarts

Shop-bought marzipan makes a clever almond base for fruit tarts. Replace strawberries with whatever's in season – thinly sliced apples, plums or apricots would be particularly good.

TAKES 40 MINUTES • MAKES 6

375g pack ready-rolled puff pastry
25g/1oz butter, melted
200g/7oz marzipan, thinly sliced
400g/14oz large strawberries, hulled and sliced
25g/1oz golden caster sugar
25g/1oz toasted flaked almonds
vanilla ice cream, to serve

1 Heat the oven to 220C/200C fan/gas 7. Unravel the pastry and prick the surface with a fork. Cut into six squares and put on a non-stick baking sheet.
2 Lightly brush the edges of the squares with a little of the melted butter and put a couple of slices of marzipan on the top of each. Lay two rows of strawberry slices down the side of each tart and a third over the gap in the middle. Drizzle the tarts with the remaining melted butter and sprinkle with sugar. Bake for about 20–25 minutes, until golden brown on the base. Scatter the toasted almonds over the top and serve warm with a scoop of vanilla ice cream.

PER TART 473 kcals, protein 7g, carboyhdrate 49g, fat 29g, sat fat 10g, fibre 3g, sugar 32g, salt 0.73g

American pecan pies

These are flavoured with bourbon, the American-style whiskey from the Kentucky area of the US. If you don't have small tart tins, you can make a large pie in a 23cm-round tin and bake it for 40 minutes.

TAKES 1 HOUR 10 MINUTES, PLUS CHILLING • MAKES 6

300g/10oz plain flour
150g/6oz melted butter
50g/2oz golden caster sugar
FOR THE FILLING
175g/6oz pecan nut halves
4 large eggs
85g/3oz light muscovado sugar
175g/6oz golden syrup
1 tsp vanilla extract
2 tbsp bourbon
50g/2oz melted butter
dollop of double cream or crème fraîche,
    to serve

1 Heat the oven to 190C/170C fan/gas 5. Work the flour, butter and sugar together with your hands until well mixed, then press on to the base and up the sides of six fluted 10cm tart tins. Put on to a baking sheet.
2 Reserve 36 pecan halves and roughly chop the rest. Beat together the eggs, sugar, syrup, vanilla, bourbon, melted butter and chopped pecans, and spoon into the tart cases. Top each one with six pecan halves, then bake for 20–25 minutes until golden and set. The filling will rise up as it bakes, but will settle back as it cools. Best served with a dollop of double cream or crème fraîche on the side.

PER PIE 871 kcals, protein 13g, carbs 89g, fat 53g, sat fat 20g, fibre 3g, sugar 50g, salt 0.87g

American pecan pies

Individual strawberry and almond tarts

Cinnamon–pecan sticky buns

Chelsea buns meet pecan pie in these sticky breakfast treats.

TAKES 1 HOUR, PLUS RISING AND COOLING • MAKES 16

450g/1lb strong white flour
50g/2oz golden caster sugar
85g/3oz cold butter, cut into small pieces
7g sachet dried yeast
2 large eggs, beaten
150ml/¼ pint full-fat milk
vegetable oil, for greasing
FOR THE FILLING
2 tsp ground cinnamon
85g/3oz light brown soft sugar
100g/3½oz pecan nuts
FOR THE TOPPING
125g/4oz melted butter, plus extra
125ml/4fl oz maple syrup
50g/2oz light brown soft sugar
100g/3½oz pecan nuts, roughly chopped

1 Mix the flour, sugar and 1 teaspoon salt, then rub in the butter to fine crumbs. Tip in the yeast, eggs and milk then mix to a soft dough. Knead for 10 minutes until elastic then tip into an oiled bowl. Cover and leave to rise for 1 hour or until doubled in size. For the filling, whizz everything in a processor until fine.

2 Knead the dough and split it in two. Roll each piece to a 25x35cm rectangle. Brush with half the melted butter, then sprinkle the filling over. Roll up from the long edge, then pinch to seal. Slice both pieces into eight.

3 Grease two 20x30cm baking sheets. Mix the remaining topping ingredients and spread over the sheets. Sit the buns on top, spacing them well apart. Cover with lightly oiled cling film and leave for 30 minutes to rise.

4 Meanwhile, heat the oven to 180C/160C fan/gas 4. Bake for 30 minutes until golden and firm. Serve warm, sticky-side up.

PER BUN 731 kcals, protein 12g, carbs 80g, fat 43g, sat fat 16g, fibre 3g, sugar 36g, salt 1.13g

Hot cross muffin buns

Cute and easy to make, these little fruity buns are sure to please at Easter time.

TAKES ABOUT 3 HOURS • MAKES 9

450g/1lb strong white bread flour, plus extra
   for dusting
50g/2oz cold butter, cut into pieces
7g sachet fast-action yeast
2 tsp ground mixed spice
50g/2oz golden caster sugar
finely grated zest 1 lemon
250ml/9fl oz milk, tepid, plus extra to glaze
2 large eggs, beaten
200g/7oz luxury mixed dried fruit, cherries
   halved
FOR THE CROSSES AND GLAZE
2 tbsp plain flour
5–6 tsp cold water
golden syrup, to glaze

1 Put the flour and ½ teaspoon salt in a bowl, and rub in the butter. Stir in the yeast, mixed spice, sugar and lemon zest, then mix in the milk and eggs. Knead for 10 minutes, then leave to rise, covered, until doubled in size, for about 1 hour.

2 Pat into a large flat circle on a lightly floured surface then tip the fruit into the middle and encase it in the dough. Knead the fruit in evenly, then shape into nine balls.

3 Cut nine 14cm squares of baking parchment and use to line a muffin tin. Drop in balls of dough. Cover with oiled cling film, then leave for 30–45 minutes or until doubled in size. Heat the oven to 200C/180C fan/gas 6.

4 Brush the buns with milk. Mix the flour and water, then pipe as crosses over the buns. Bake for 15 minutes or until golden. Brush with golden syrup while warm.

PER BUN 352 kcals, protein 10g, carbs 65g, fat 8g, sat fat 4g, fibre 2g, added sugar 8g, salt 0.54g

Hot cross muffin buns

Cinnamon–pecan sticky buns

Little blueberry cream tarts

These dainty tarts would be wonderful for tea, or as a special dessert.

TAKES 35–45 MINUTES • MAKES 24

100g/3½oz butter, softened
100g/3½oz golden caster sugar
100g/3½oz blanched hazelnuts, finely ground
   in a food processor
250g tub mascarpone
2–3 tbsp milk
3 tbsp good-quality lemon curd
FOR THE TOPPING
25g/1oz golden caster sugar
2 x 125g punnets blueberries

1 Heat the oven to 180C/160C fan/gas 4. Beat the butter and sugar together with a wooden spoon until soft and creamy. Mix in the hazelnuts.
2 Put a heaped teaspoon of the mixture into the wells of two 12-hole non-stick muffin tins. Bake for 10 minutes until golden and slightly risen. Cool for 5 minutes until firm, then ease each tart from the tins with a small knife.
3 For the topping, gently dissolve the sugar in 1 tablespoon of water in a pan set over a medium heat, then bring to the boil for 30 seconds only. Off the heat, tip in the blueberries. Stir, then cool.
4 Beat the mascarpone with the milk to make a soft creamy mix. Ripple in the lemon curd. Spoon a little mascarpone mixture into each tart case, then spoon over a few of the syrupy blueberries.

PER TART 179 kcals, protein 1g, carbs 11g, fat 15g, sat fat 7g, fibre 1g, added sugar 8g, salt 0.15g

Warm chocolate and macadamia nut tarts

The only rule with these tarts is to eat them straight from the oven while the centres are still gooey.

TAKES 1 HOUR, PLUS CHILLING • MAKES 4

375g pack sweet pastry
200g/7oz dark chocolate, broken into pieces
2 tbsp double cream
1 tbsp Disaronno or brandy (optional)
2 large eggs, plus 1 yolk
50g/2oz caster sugar
85g/3oz macadamia nuts, chopped
icing sugar, to dust

1 Roll the pastry out to a £1 coin thickness then use to line four tartlet cases (about 10 x 3cm). Trim the excess then freeze for 30 minutes. Heat the oven to 190C/170C fan/gas 5. Line the cases with parchment and baking beans, then cook on a baking sheet for 15 minutes. Remove the beans and paper, then cook for 3–5 minutes more until the pastry is pale golden and biscuity.
2 Melt the chocolate, cream and alcohol, if using, in a heatproof bowl over a pan of barely simmering water. Whisk the eggs, yolk and sugar until light and frothy. Briefly whisk the melted chocolate into the eggs and fold through most of the chopped macadamia nuts.
3 Fill the cases with the chocolate mix, scatter with the remaining nuts then bake for 12 minutes. The tops of the tarts will soufflé up and they should still be soft in the middle. Serve straight away, dusted with icing sugar.

PER TART 867 kcals, protein 12g, carbs 77g, fat 59g, sat fat 18g, fibre 4g, sugar 53g, salt 0.5g

Little blueberry cream tarts

Warm chocolate and macadamia nut tarts

Blackberry and apple pasties

Just a handful of ingredients make a deliciously easy twist on apple pie.

TAKES 35 MINUTES • MAKES 4

icing sugar, to dust
425g pack ready-rolled shortcrust pastry
2 Bramley apples, peeled, cored and chopped
2 tbsp light brown soft sugar
150g punnet blackberries
thick cream, to serve

1 Heat the oven to 200C/180C fan/gas 6. Dust a work surface with icing sugar, then unroll the pastry and cut out four rounds using a small side plate as a template.
2 Combine the apples and sugar with the blackberries, and put a small pile on each pastry circle. Dampen the edge of the pastry, then fold over to encase the fruit. Pinch and fold over the pastry along one edge to make a pasty shape. Slash each pasty three times, lift on to a baking sheet and bake for around 20 minutes or until puffed and golden. Serve with cream.

PER PASTY 471 kcals, protein 7g, carbs 58g, fat 25g, sat fat 10g, fibre 3g, sugar 20g, salt 0.85g

Hot sugared doughnuts

Deliciously golden, light doughnuts and not a deep-fryer in sight.

TAKES 45 MINUTES, PLUS RISING AND COOLING • MAKES 20

250g/9oz plain flour, plus extra for kneading
½ x 7g sachet fast-action yeast
50g/2oz golden caster sugar, plus 50g/2oz extra for coating
2 large egg yolks
150ml/¼ pint milk, warmed
50g/2oz butter, melted, plus 50g/2oz extra for coating
370g jar raspberry jam

1 Mix the flour, yeast, sugar and ½ teaspoon salt in a large bowl. Beat the yolks, milk and butter together, and stir into the flour mix to make a dough. Leave to stand for 10 minutes.
2 Lightly flour a work surface then knead the dough for about 5 minutes until smooth and springy. Leave to rise in an oiled, covered bowl in a warm place for about 2 hours.
3 Knead once or twice then shape into walnut-size balls and put on baking sheets, well spaced. Cover again, then leave to rise for 30 minutes–1 hour until risen and pillowy. Heat the oven to 190C/170C fan/gas 5.
4 Bake for 12–15 minutes until risen and dark golden. Melt the extra butter in a pan and put the extra sugar into a large bowl. Cool the doughnuts for a few minutes, then brush with the melted butter and roll in sugar. Pipe in jam using a 5mm nozzle or serve warm with jam for dipping.

PER DOUGHNUT 135 kcals, protein 2g, carbs 18g, fat 7g, sat fat 3g, fibre none, sugar 8g, salt 0.21g

Spiced apple filo parcels

Apple strudel is served for afternoon tea all over Germany and Austria. Go on, try these with a cup of coffee and a dollop of cream.

TAKES 40 MINUTES, PLUS COOLING • MAKES 6

3 dessert apples, peeled, cored and finely chopped
zest and juice ½ lemon
50g/2oz sultanas
1 tbsp light muscovado sugar
½ tsp ground mixed spice
6 large sheets filo pastry, each about 48 x 30cm
40g/1½oz butter, melted
sesame seeds, for sprinkling

1 Heat the oven to 200C/180C fan/gas 6. Put the apples, lemon zest and juice, sultanas, sugar and spice in a frying pan. Cook covered on a low heat for 8–10 minutes until the apples are tender. Cool slightly.

2 Lightly brush a sheet of pastry with butter (keep spare pastry covered). Fold lengthways into three, making one long piece. Put a spoonful of the mixture 4cm from the top short edge. Fold top left corner to the right, making a triangle over the filling. Keep folding into a parcel. Repeat with the remaining pastry and filling.

3 Put the parcels on a lightly greased baking sheet; brush with a little butter. Sprinkle over a few sesame seeds and bake for around 15 minutes or until golden. Serve warm.

PER PARCEL 246 kcals, protein 4g, carbs 42g, fat 8g, sat fat 4g, fibre 2g, added sugar 4g, salt 1.17g

Rhubarb crumble puffs

This recipe makes four dessert-size portions, but you could make eight small tarts for tea instead. Just give them a few minutes less in the oven.

TAKES 30–35 MINUTES • MAKES 4

5 rhubarb sticks, cut into 3cm pieces
1 tsp ground cinnamon
3 tbsp plain flour, plus extra for rolling
5 tbsp light brown soft sugar
½ x 500g block puff pastry
3 tbsp unsalted butter
50g/2oz rolled oats

1 Heat the oven to 200C/180C fan/gas 6. In a bowl, toss the rhubarb with cinnamon, 1 tablespoon of the flour and 2 tablespoons of the sugar. Line a baking sheet with baking parchment. Roll out the pastry on a floured surface to about 20x30cm, then cut into quarters and put on the sheet.

2 Rub together the remaining flour and sugar, the butter and oats to make a rough crumble mixture. Divide the rhubarb among the pastry quarters, leaving a 1cm rim. Sprinkle the oat mixture over, then fold and pinch each corner to keep the filling in. Bake for 20–25 minutes, then serve warm.

PER PUFF 465 kcals, protein 6g, carbs 53g, fat 27g, sat fat 13g, fibre 3g, sugar 21g, salt 0.57g

Pecan tassies

The pastry for these pies is very unusual and completely delicious. Made with cream cheese, it's light, crumbly and doesn't need rolling out.

**TAKES 40 MINUTES, PLUS COOLING •
MAKES 12**

85g/3oz pecan nuts, toasted
1 egg yolk
50g/2oz light brown soft sugar
2 tbsp maple syrup
½ tsp vanilla extract
15g/½oz butter, melted
cream and maple syrup, to serve
FOR THE PASTRY
50g/2oz pecan nuts
50g/2oz full-fat soft cheese
50g/2oz butter, softened
50g/2oz plain flour, plus extra for dusting

1 For the pastry, whizz the pecans in a food processor until finely ground then pulse in the remaining ingredients with a pinch of salt just until the dough comes together. Lightly flour your hands, then roll the dough into 12 small balls. Use your fingers to gently press them into the bottom and up the sides of a 12-hole mini-muffin tin. Chill for 10 minutes.
2 Heat the oven to 180C/160C fan/gas 4. Reserve 12 toasted pecans then roughly chop the rest. Whisk together the remaining ingredients with a pinch of salt. Stir in the chopped pecans.
3 Bake the cases for 5 minutes – gently press down with a teaspoon if the pastry puffs up a little. Spoon 1–2 teaspoons of filling into each case and top with a reserved pecan. Bake for 15–20 minutes until golden and set. Cool a little in the tin then eat warm with cream and maple syrup.

PER PIE 173 kcals, protein 2g, carbs 10g, fat 14g, sat fat 4g, fibre 1g, sugar 7g, salt 0.13g

Devonshire splits

Light and puffy, Devonshire splits are the ultimate nostalgic teatime treat. Enjoy this easy recipe with strawberry jam and clotted cream.

TAKES 45 MINUTES, PLUS RISING • MAKES 12

600g/1lb 5oz strong white bread flour, plus
    extra for dusting
50g/2oz butter at room temperature,
    cut into pieces
7g sachet fast-action yeast
2 tsp caster sugar
400ml/14fl oz full-fat milk, warmed
strawberry jam
2 x 113g pots clotted cream
icing sugar, for dusting

1 Put the flour and butter in a large bowl and rub into fine crumbs. Stir in the yeast, 1 teaspoon salt and the sugar. Stir in the milk to make a soft dough. Knead on a floured surface for 10 minutes; sprinkle with flour if it sticks. Put the dough in a large buttered bowl and cover with cling film. Leave in a warm place for 50 minutes–1 hour.
2 Knead briefly, then cut into 12 even pieces. Keep the dough covered as you shape the rolls into rounds. Put on to two greased baking sheets.
3 Cover again then leave to rise for 40–50 minutes, depending on the room temperature. Meanwhile, heat the oven to 220C/200C fan/gas 7.
4 Bake for 15–20 minutes until pale golden. Cool on a wire rack. When cold, cut at an angle with a serrated knife. Spread with jam and clotted cream and dust with icing sugar.

PER SPLIT 366 kcals, protein 7g, carbs 48g, fat 17g, sat fat 11g, fibre 2g, added sugar 8g, salt 0.56g

Pecan tassies

Devonshire splits

Classic cherry and almond slice

Everyone will love this tasty bake with its Bakewell-like filling and layer of tangy cherry jam.

TAKES 1 HOUR, PLUS COOLING • MAKES 16

375g pack ready-rolled shortcrust pastry
100g/3½oz butter, softened
100g/3½oz golden caster sugar
1 large egg, beaten
25g/1oz ground rice
50g/2oz ground almonds
50g/2oz desiccated coconut
50g/2oz walnuts, roughly chopped
5 tbsp cherry jam
100g/3½oz undyed glacé cherries

1 Heat the oven to 180C/160C fan/gas 4 and line the base of an 18x27cm (or thereabouts) baking tin with greaseproof paper. Line the base and sides with the pastry, trim the edges, then chill while you make the filling.
2 Beat the butter and sugar together until fluffy, then gradually add the egg until creamy. Stir in the ground rice, almonds, coconut and nuts. Spread the jam over the pastry, then dollop the almond mix on top. Don't worry if there are some little gaps as the filling will spread during baking.
3 Dot the cherries over the top, then bake for 40–45 minutes until light golden and set. Check after 30 minutes – if the top is browning too quickly, cover loosely with greaseproof paper. Cool in the tin; cut into 16 slices.

PER SLICE 275 kcals, protein 3g, carbs 27g, fat 18g, sat fat 8g, fibre 1g, sugar 15g, salt 0.36g

Walnut and rosewater baklava

These little pastries are particularly good with a strong cup of coffee at the end of a meal.

TAKES 35 MINUTES, PLUS COOLING • MAKES 16

FOR THE SYRUP
140g/5oz caster sugar
250ml/9fl oz hot water
2 tbsp rosewater
FOR THE LAYERS
100g/3½oz butter, melted, plus extra for greasing
200g/7oz walnuts, finely chopped
50g/2oz caster sugar
1 heaped tsp ground cinnamon
½ tsp ground cloves
400g pack filo pastry (you will need 12 sheets)

1 For the syrup, dissolve the sugar in the water in a pan over a low heat, then boil for 15 minutes, or until thickened but not coloured. Stir in the rosewater and set aside to cool.
2 Meanwhile, lightly butter a 15x25cm baking sheet and mix the walnuts, sugar and spices together. Unroll the pastry, peel off 12 sheets and, keeping the layers together, cut a rectangle just big enough to fit inside the tin. Re-wrap any leftover pastry for another time.
3 Heat the oven to 180C/160C fan/gas 4. Brush four pastry sheets with the melted butter and use them to cover the bottom of the baking sheet. Top with half of the nut mix then repeat, using four sheets of buttered pastry for each layer and finishing with a layer of pastry. Using a sharp knife, cut diagonal lines all the way through to create 16 small diamonds. Bake for 15–20 minutes until golden. Pour the syrup over, then cool.

PER DIAMOND 169 kcals, protein 2g, carbs 16g, fat 11g, sat fat 3g, fibre 0.3g, added sugar 11g, salt 0.29g

Walnut and rosewater baklava

Classic cherry and almond slice

Orange, cranberry and almond mince pies

These are just as delicious as traditional mince pies, but a little lighter.

TAKES 35 MINUTES, PLUS CHILLING ● MAKES 24

200g/7oz very cold butter, cubed
400g/14oz plain flour, plus extra for dusting
100g/3½oz golden caster sugar
100g/3½oz ground almonds
zest 2 oranges
2 tbsp milk (or use fresh orange juice)
100g/3½oz frozen cranberries
410g jar good-quality mincemeat
handful of flaked almonds
2 tsp icing sugar, plus extra to dust
200ml pot crème fraîche, to serve

1 Put the butter and flour into a food processor, then whizz until the butter has disappeared. Pulse in the sugar, almonds and half the orange zest. Add the milk or orange juice and pulse to a rough dough. Tip on to the work surface, press together and shape into a smooth disk. Chill for 15 minutes.
2 Roll out the dough on a floured surface to the thickness of a £1 coin. Using an 8cm cutter, stamp out 24 circles, and use to line the wells of two 12-hole bun tins.
3 Heat the oven to 200C/180C fan/gas 6. Mix the cranberries and mincemeat, then spoon into the cases. Scatter each pie with a few flaked almonds. Bake for 18–20 minutes until the pastry and almonds are golden. Stir the icing sugar and remaining zest into the crème fraîche. Dust the tarts with the extra icing sugar and serve with the crème fraîche.

PER PIE 213 kcals, protein 3g, carbs 29g, fat 10g, sat fat 5g, fibre 2g, sugar 14g, salt 0.14g

Festive muffin tarts

The perfect sweet offering for the holiday period: fruity and spicy but without any mincemeat.

TAKES 1 HOUR 20 MINUTES ● MAKES 24

450g/1lb plain flour, plus extra for rolling
250g/9oz cold salted butter, cut into small pieces
25g/1oz ground almonds
50g/2oz golden caster sugar
1 egg yolk, beaten
FOR THE FILLING
300g/10oz ground almonds
250g/9oz golden caster sugar
100g/3½oz currants
100g/3½oz sultanas
50g/2oz flaked almonds
2 tsp ground cinnamon
1 tsp ground nutmeg
1 tsp ground mixed spice
200g/7oz butter, melted
4 large eggs, beaten
finely grated zest and juice 1 lemon and 1 orange
icing sugar, for dusting

1 First, make the pastry. Measure 150ml/¼ pint water in a jug. Rub together the flour and butter until the mixture looks like crumbs. Stir in the ground almonds and sugar then add the yolk and a little of the water, stirring with a knife. Gradually work in the rest of the water, stirring until you have a soft pastry ball. Chill for 30 minutes.
2 Heat the oven to 200C/180C fan/gas 6. For the filling, mix the dry ingredients in a large bowl. Stir in the butter, eggs, orange and lemon zests and juice.
3 Roll out the pastry on a lightly floured surface to about 5mm thickness. Cut out 24 rounds with a 10cm-round cutter. Line two 12-hole muffin tins, spoon in the filling then bake for 20–25 minutes until pale golden. Turn out on to a wire rack and dust with icing sugar. Lovely served warm or cold.

PER TART 394 kcals, protein 7g, carbs 36g, fat 26g, sat fat 11g, fibre 2g, added sugar none, salt 0.41g

Orange, cranberry and almond mince pies

Festive muffin tarts

Mincemeat custard pies

These are so quick, plus you get all the different textures and flavours in each mouthful.

TAKES 20 MINUTES • MAKES 16–18

2 x 150g pots Devon custard
6 level tbsp ground almonds
375g pack ready-rolled puff pastry
16–18 tsp mincemeat (about a 410g jar)
flaked almonds, for scattering
icing sugar, for dusting

1 Heat the oven to 220C/200C fan/gas 7. Stir the custard and almonds together.
2 Unroll the pastry, then cut out circles using a 7cm round plain cutter. Gather up the pastry trimmings, re-roll, then cut out more circles – you should get 16–18. Use to line a couple of muffin tins.
3 Spoon a heaped teaspoon of the custard mix into each tart case, then top with a scant teaspoon of mincemeat. Scatter over some flaked almonds, then bake for 10 minutes until puffy and golden. Cool briefly in the tins, then dust with icing sugar and serve still slightly warm.

PER PIE (for 16) 169 kcals, protein 4g, carbs 16g, fat 11g, sat fat 3g, fibre 1g, sugar 7g, salt 0.22g

Stollen buns

These make a great present or a sweet little something for the children to take around to neighbours at Christmas time.

TAKES 1 HOUR, PLUS RISING • MAKES 14

500g/1lb 2oz strong white bread flour, plus extra for dusting
3 tbsp light muscovado sugar
7g sachet fast-action yeast
3 tsp ground mixed spice
1 tsp salt
85g/3oz butter
200ml/7fl oz milk, plus 1 tbsp to glaze
1 tbsp black treacle
2 tbsp brandy
2 large eggs
2 tbsp sunflower or vegetable oil
250g mix sultanas, raisins, peel and chopped glacé cherries
zest 1 orange and 1 lemon
400g/14oz white marzipan
handful of flaked almonds
FOR THE SYRUP
50g/2oz icing sugar mixed with 4 tbsp hot water

1 Mix the first five ingredients in a large bowl. Rub in the butter. Warm the milk, treacle and brandy, then beat in one egg and the oil, and mix into the bowl. Set aside for 10 minutes, then briefly knead on a floured surface. Cover and leave to rise until doubled in size.
2 Roll the dough to A4 size. Scatter over the dried fruit and zests, then knead until even. Roll to about 50x15cm. Dampen the edges. Roll the marzipan to a 50cm sausage, then roll the dough around it. Pinch to seal.
3 Heat the oven to 200C/180C fan/gas 6. Slice the dough into 14, discarding the very ends. Flatten a little, then put on to lined baking sheets, well spaced. Re-cover and rise until pillowy. Beat the remaining egg with the extra tablespoon of milk and use to glaze. Sprinkle with almonds. Bake for 15 minutes. Generously brush the syrup over the buns.

PER BUN 407 Kcals, protein 8g, carbs 68g, fat 13g, sat fat 4g, fibre 2g, sugar 41g, salt 0.55g

Chunky mince pie slices

These appealing little slices make a lighter, really fruity alternative to mince pies.

TAKES 35 MINUTES • MAKES 15

300g/10oz mincemeat
25g/1oz pecan nuts, mix of broken and whole
25g/1oz pistachio nuts, halved lengthways
2 tbsp flaked almonds
25g/1oz dried cranberries
½ small apple, peeled, cored and finely chopped
finely grated zest 1 lemon, plus 2 tsp juice
375g ready-rolled sheet puff pastry
1 rounded tbsp ground almonds
50g/2oz icing sugar

1 Heat the oven to 220C/200C fan/gas 7. Combine the mincemeat with the nuts, cranberries, apple and lemon zest.
2 Unroll the pastry on to a floured work surface. Slice off a strip across one end to leave a 23cm/9in square of pastry. Cut out 15–30 star shapes from the strip, thinly re-rolling the trimmings until it is all used up.
3 Lay the pastry square on a baking sheet and scatter over the ground almonds. Spread the mincemeat mixture over so that it comes right to the edge of the pastry. Lay the stars in lines across the mincemeat, slightly overlapping them to fit, if necessary, so that you can cut out 15 slices when baked.
4 Bake for 15 minutes or until the pastry is golden. Leave to cool. Mix the icing sugar with 2 teaspoons lemon juice. Drizzle over the cool pastry and cut into 15 slices.

PER SLICE 204 kcals, protein 3g, carbs 27g, fat 10g, sat fat 3g, fibre 1g, sugar 17g, salt 0.21g

Festive mince pies

Top with marzipan stars or meringue before baking to vary these little celebratory pies.

TAKES 40 MINUTES, PLUS 30 MINUTES CHILLING TIME • MAKES 18

FOR THE PASTRY
200g/7oz plain flour
50g/2oz ground almonds
140g/5oz butter, chopped into small pieces
grated rind 1 orange
50g/2oz caster sugar
1 egg yolk
FOR THE FILLING AND DECORATION
200g/7oz mincemeat
1 egg white, lightly whisked
caster sugar, for dusting

1 Heat the oven to 200C/180C fan/gas 6. Whizz the flour, almonds, butter, orange rind and sugar into crumbs. Add the egg yolk and a teaspoon of cold water and pulse until it forms a dough. Wrap in cling film and chill for 30 minutes.
2 Roll out the dough thinly and stamp out 18 x 7.5cm/3in rounds. Use to line bun tins. Put a heaped teaspoon of mincemeat in each pastry case. Stamp out nine more pastry rounds. Cut out festive shapes from the centre of each round.
3 Cover the pies with the shapes and pastry rounds with the centres removed. Brush the tops with egg white and dust lightly with caster sugar. Bake for 12–15 minutes until the pastry is crisp and golden. Cool in the tins for 5 minutes, then cool fully on a wire rack.

PER PIE 164 kcals, protein 2g, carbs 20g, fat 9g, sat fat 5g, fibre 1g, added sugar 9g, salt 0.17g

Index

Picture credits

BBC *Good Food* magazine and BBC Books would like to thank the following people for providing photos. While every effort has been made to trace and acknowledge all photographers, we should like to apologise should their be any errors or omissions.

2 Lis Parsons; 8 Linda Burgess; 11t Linda Burgess; 11b Craig Robertson; 13t Craig Robertson; 13b Roger Stowell; 15t Marie-Louise Avery; 15b Philip Webb; 19t Roger Stowell; 19b David Munns; 21t Roger Stowell; 21b Philip Webb; 23t Linda Burgess; 23b Roger Stowell; 27t Martin Brigdale; 27b David Munns; 29t Ian Wallace; 29b David Munns; 31t David Munns; 31b Howard Shooter; 35t Philip Webb; 35b Michael Paul; 37t Marie-Louise Avery; 37b Simon Wheeler; 39t Philip Webb; 39b Philip Webb; 41t Roger Stowell; 41b Michael Paul; 42 Roger Stowell; 45t Gus Filgate; 45b Jean Cazals; 47t Michael Paul; 47b Tim Young; 51t Linda Burgess; 53t Linda Burgess; 53b Philip Webb; 55t Roger Stowell; 55b Simon Wheeler; 59t Linda Burgess; 59b Michael Paul; 61t Michael Paul; 61b Tim Young; 43t Philip Webb; 43b David Munns; 67t Marie-Louise Avery; 67b Lis Parsons; 69t Mary-Louise Avery; 69b Gareth Morgans; 71t Philip Webb; 71b Philip Webb; 72 Roger Stowell; 75t Roger Stowell; 75b Simon Wheeler; 77t Peter Cassidy; 77b Philip Webb; 79t Philip Webb; 79b Anna Hodgson; 83t Lis Parsons; 83b Lis Parsons; 85t Philip Webb; 85b Geoff Wilkinson; 87t Tim Young; 87b David Munns; 91t Philip Webb; 93t Yuki Sugiura; 93b Lis Parsons; 95t Martin Thompson; 95b Simon Wheeler; Gareth 99t Morgans; 99b David Munns; 101t Adrian Taylor; 101b Jean Cazals; 103t Lis Parsons; 103b David Munns; 107t Michelle Garrett; 107b Myles New; 109t Marie-Louise Avery; 109b Lis Parsons; 111t Lis Parsons; 111b Gareth Morgans; 115t David Munns; 115b Peter Cassidy; 117t Myles New; 117b Myles New; 118 Roger Stowell; 121t Simon Wheeler; 121b David Munns; 123t Jonathan Wheeler; 125b Lis Parsons; 127t Marie-Louise Avery; 127b Michael Paul; 129t Simon Wheeler; 129b Tim Young; 131t Jean Cazals; 131b Roger Stowell; 133t David Munns; 133b Simon Wheeler; 135t David Munns; 135b William Lingwood; 137t Gus Filgate; 137b Philip Webb; 139t Gareth Morgans; 139b Roger Stowell; 141t Lis Parsons; 141b Elizabeth Zeschin; 143t Dawie Verwey; 143b Simon Smith; 145t Lis Parsons; 145b Philip Webb; 147t Philip Webb; 147b Lis Parsons; 148 Philip Webb; 151t Philip Webb; 151b Philip Webb; 155t David Munns; 155b Philip Webb; 157t Jonathan Whittaker; 157b Marie-Louise Avery; 159t Simon Wheeler; 159b Simon Wheeler; 161t Simon Wheeler; 161b Philip Webb; 165t Noel Murphy; 165b Philip Webb; 167t Roger Stowell; 167b Philip Webb; 169b Gareth Morgans; 170 Marie-Louise Avery; 173t Geoff Wilkinson; 173b Myles New; 175t Marie-Louise Avery; 175b David Munns; 177t Roger Stowell; 177b Marie-Louise Avery; 179t David Munns; 179b Myles New; 183b Simon Wheeler; 185t Steve Baxter; 185b Myles New; 187t Myles New; 187b Simon Wheeler.